THE
LITTLE
BOOK
OF
NORFOLK

NEIL R. STOREY

The History Press

For all my friends at FOND – Friends of Norfolk Dialect.

First published 2011

The History Press
The Mill, Brimscombe Port
Stroud, Gloucestershire, GL5 2QG
www.thehistorypress.co.uk

British Library Cataloguing in Publication Data.
A catalogue record for this book is available from the British Library.

ISBN 978 0 7524 6160 1
Typesetting and origination by The History Press
Printed in Great Britain

CONTENTS

INTRODUCTION

Norfolk is a remarkable and truly beautiful county where most feel a very keen sense of place and identity, be they visitor, new resident or local. In such a diverse and historic part of East Anglia, folks soon feel they 'know' the county but there is always something new to discover, be it fascinating, frivolous or even bizarre. This book does not pretend to be a history, concise almanac or guide to the county, instead it is a collection of the ephemeral and miscellaneous facts about Norfolk you didn't know you wanted to know until now. The contents of this volume will enliven conversation or quiz and leave even those who know and love Norfolk with the 'well fancy that!' factor or, as some may say, 'blass me thass a rummun!' Things like . . .

The geographical centre of Norfolk is in East Dereham Tesco's car park.

James Brooke (1803–68), the first white Rajah of Sarawak received a brief education at the Norwich School, from which he ran away.

Famous Victorian writer Wilkie Collins, author of *The Woman in White* and *The Moonstone*, visited Winterton in 1864 while researching his novel *Armadale* and fell in love with local girl Martha Rudd. She returned to London with Collins where they lived as husband and wife under the name Mr and Mrs William Dawson and had three children together.

Davros, creator of the Daleks, lives in Bawburgh.

The biggest explosion during the English Civil War took place in Norwich on Monday 24 April 1648.

When Wehrmacht Field Marshals Karl Gerd von Rundstedt and Erich von Manstein were released from captivity in July 1948, they left for Germany from Diss.

The Anglia Television knight was originally a trophy commissioned by King William III of the Netherlands in 1850 as a sports club trophy.

And my personal favourite . . .

The priceless golden torc ploughed up on Ken Kill at Snettisham in 1948, described by the British Museum as 'the most famous object from Iron Age Britain', was initially discarded as part of an old bedstead and lay by the side of the field for about a week before it was reconsidered.

See the ease with which one can enliven conversation, impress and intrigue with facts obtained from this book.

Neil R. Storey, 2011

1

TOPOGRAPHY

ABOUT THE COUNTY

By the fifth century the Angles, after whom East Anglia and England itself are named, had established control of the eastern region and later became the 'north folk' and the 'south folk', hence, 'Norfolk' and 'Suffolk'.

The first definite record of the place name Northwic (the earliest name for Norwich) appears on coins of Aethelstan I of England minted between AD 920 and 940.

The Domesday Book shows that during the eleventh century Norfolk was one of the most heavily populated counties and this remained the case until 1600.

Norwich is the most easterly city in the United Kingdom.

Norfolk is officially the driest county in the UK.

Dragon Hall on the ancient King Street in Norwich is the only known surviving medieval merchant's trading hall in Western Europe.

The returns of the Secret Committee during the nineteenth century showed Norfolk 'amongst the most loyal counties in the kingdom.'

Norfolk is the largest of the eastern counties, it is the fifth largest metropolitan county of England with an area of 537,070 hectares (2,074 square miles) and measures 68 miles from east to west and 41 miles from north to south.

There are 6,329 miles of roads and 250 miles of waterways in the county.

Norfolk was divided into 33 Hundreds consisting of 540 parishes. The Norfolk Hundreds were: Blofield, Brothercross, Clackclose, Clavering, Depwade, Diss, Earsham, North Erpingham, South Erpingham, Eynesford, East Flegg, West Flegg, Forehoe, Freebridge-Lynn, Freebridge-Marshland, Gallow, North Greenhoe, South Greenhoe, Grimshoe, Guiltcross, Happing, Henstead, Holt, Humbleyard, Launditch, Loddon, Mitford, Shropham, Smithdon, Taverham, Tunstead, Walsham and Wayland.

The historic Norfolk Hundreds were replaced by the four districts of North, South, East and West Norfolk in 1974.

By the sixteenth century Norwich had grown to become the second largest city in England but over one-third of the population died during a plague epidemic in 1579.

Over 25 per cent of people in Norfolk live within 8 miles of Norwich Castle.

The medieval Wayland Wood near Watton is said to be the setting for the story 'Babes in the Wood'.

Historian and naturalist William George Clarke coined the term 'Breckland' in 1894.

Research by the East of England Tourist Board estimated that in 2007 there were 4,220,000 staying visitors in Norfolk. The total number of day visitors was estimated at 25,631,000.

The village of Upper Sheringham has one of the greatest reputations for longevity of its residents in Britain; in fact, one in five Norfolk residents are aged over 65 and one in ten is aged 75 and over.

Worstead has a large market place but no market. Granted by ancient right, markets were held on Saturdays until the plague visited the village in 1666 and the market moved to North Walsham, never to return.

The good quality and reputation of Aylsham linens and Aylsham canvases were nationally renowned in the fourteenth century.

King's Lynn was known for many years as Bishop's Lynn. After the Dissolution Henry VIII claimed the properties and rights of the religious houses and granted a second charter in 1536, but seeing the name of the town as rather incongruous after his seizures, changed it to Lynn Regis (King's Lynn).

There are only two place names in Norfolk that begin with the letter 'Q': Quidenham (10 miles north-west of Thetford) and Quarles (4 miles south-west of Wells).

An arch once straddled the road at Westwick between two lodge houses. Built in about 1780 it marked the entrance to the Westwick estate and was used as a dove cote. When the Norwich to North Walsham turnpike was diverted through the estate, the road was diverted to pass under it. By 1981 the arch had become structurally unsound and was demolished amid great controversy.

Architect George Skipper's masterpiece, the Royal Arcade in Norwich, which opened on 25 May 1899, was built on the site of the old Royal Hotel, hence its 'Royal' appellation.

A time ball erected on the north-west angle of the battlements of Norwich Castle to announce Greenwich time every day at 10.00 a.m. was heard for the first time on 10 August 1900.

There are 120 round tower churches in Norfolk; more than any other county.

The first council estate to be built outside London was begun at Mile Cross, Norwich, in 1918.

When May Savage's fifteenth-century house was scheduled for demolition at Ware in Hertfordshire in 1970, she had it taken down and rebuilt it brick by brick and beam by beam at Wells-next-the-Sea. Despite being in her sixties or seventies and having no previous experience of building or construction, May carried out most of the work herself.

CRADLE OF CIVILISATION

In July 2010 archaeologists digging near the village of Happisburgh discovered 78 pieces of razor-sharp flint shaped into primitive cutting and piercing tools. They were believed to have been laid down by hunter-gatherers of the human species *Homo antecessor* some 840,000–950,000 years ago, making them the oldest human artefacts ever found in Britain.

THE POPULATION OF NORWICH

1693	29,911	1891	100,964
1752	36,369	1931	126,207
1786	40,061	1971	121,688
1821	50,173	2008	137,300
1861	74,414		

PLACE NAMES YOU DON'T EXPECT TO FIND IN NORFOLK

California (near Hemsby)
Frankfort (Sloley)
Little London (Griston)
Little Switzerland (Wroxham)
Quebec Road (East Dereham)

Shangri La (Ludham)
White City (Titchwell)
Pleasure Island (Hickling Broad)
Ciudad Rodrigo (Long Stratton)

ECCENTRIC NORFOLK PLACE NAMES

Misery Corner (Denton)
High and Low Bridge (Horstead)
Hills and Holes Plantation (Wroxham)
Lamb's Holes (Hainford)
Loke Wiffens (Hethersett)
Runcton Bottom (South Runcton)
Slubberdike Wood (Stow Bardolph)
The Gongs (North Wootton)
Gogg's Whins (Dersingham)
Vinegar Middle (North Wootton)
Puny Drain (Setchey)
Lolly Moor (East Dereham)
Nowhere (Acle)
Whinny Hills (Felthorpe)
Bingles Turn (Hevingham)
Tuzzy Muzzy (Shropham)

AND SOME ECCENTRIC STREET NAMES

Cockey Lane in Norwich was formally accorded its new name of
    London Street in January 1829
Gropekunte Lane (now Opie Street, Norwich)
Rampant Horse Street (Norwich)
Cat's Pit Lane (North Walsham)
Laughing Image Corner (Great Yarmouth)
Hangman's Lane (now Heigham Street, Norwich)
Pullover Road (West Lynn)
Dick Fool's Lane (Wendling)
Slutshole Lane (Besthorpe)
Cucumber Corner (Beighton)
Spong Road (Limpenhoe)
Nobb's Lane (Woodton)
Bloodslat Lane (Bromholme)
Long John Hill (Lakenham)
Nowhere Lane (Wereham)
Drudge Road (Gorleston)

NORFOLK PLACE NAMES TO MAKE YOU THINK TWICE

Three Cocked Hat (Maypole Green)
Swaffham Plashes (Swaffham)
The Lizard (Wymondham)
Big Bog (Sutton)
The Pulk (Hoveton)
Cess (Martham)
Potspoon Hole (Coltishall)
Dirty Lane (Swanton Morley)
Prickly Grove (Howe)
Crinkle Hill (Horsey)
Calfpightle Clump (Stockton)
Fustyweed (Lyng)
Bumwell Hill (Carleton Rode)
Tud Lane (Honingham)

THE SMALLEST, LARGEST, OLDEST, SHORTEST & HIGHEST

The smallest National Trust property in Norfolk is a section of the old Cawston Heath upon which stands the Duel Stone. It marks the spot where Sir Henry Hobart of Blickling Hall fell, mortally wounded, during a duel with Oliver le Neve of Great Witchingham on 20 August 1698.

Thetford Castle has the highest Norman motte in England, but no trace remains of the castle that once surmounted it are visible today.

The first printed map of Norfolk appeared in Christopher Saxton's *An Atlas of England and Wales* published in 1579.

The highest point in Norfolk is Beacon Hill near West Runton; it stands 338ft above sea level.

The second highest point in Norfolk at 331ft above sea level is at Pigg's Grave at Swanton Novers.

The largest village green in the county is at Old Buckenham.

The two shortest place names in the county have just three letters: Oby (10 miles north-west of Yarmouth) and Hoe (2 miles north of Dereham).

Norfolk has 659 medieval churches, the greatest concentration of such religious buildings in Northern Europe.

The narrowest of the old Yarmouth Rows was Kittywitches Row (Row 95) that was just 27in wide at its west end. The widest Yarmouth Row was Gun Row (Row 125), that stood 9ft wide in places.

The round tower of the church of St Andrew at East Lexham near Swaffham is 1,000 years old and is the oldest Saxon tower in England. The 160ft tower of the church of St Peter and St Paul at Cromer is the tallest surviving church tower in Norfolk. The 120ft tower of St Giles' Church is the highest in Norwich. Soaring above them all is the tower of Norwich Cathedral at 315ft; it is the second highest spire in England (the tallest being Salisbury Catherdral).

The largest church in Norwich is St Peter Mancroft, built between 1430 and 1455.

The world's largest rock shop is Docwras Rock Shop, Great Yarmouth, who make and sell over 80,000 sticks of rock a week.

The earliest known reference to a barber in England was John Belton, a Norwich barber recorded as resident in the city in 1163.

At almost 80ft from the ground to the top of the cap plus the reach of the sails beyond that, Sutton windmill near Stalham is the county's tallest extant windmill and one of the tallest mills in the country.

Norwich Cathedral has over a thousand carved roof bosses. Each boss is decorated with a theological image. The nave vault shows the history of the world from the creation; the cloister includes series showing the life of Christ and the Apocalypse. The roof bosses of Norwich Cathedral have been described as 'without parallel in the Christian world.'

TEN NORFOLK CASTLES & FORTS

Warham Camp: An Iron Age hillfort probably built by the Iceni.

Burgh Castle: One of several Roman forts constructed as a defence against Saxon raiders.

Castle Acre Castle: Founded shortly after the Norman Conquest of 1066 by William de Warenne.

Buckenham Castle: A Norman castle built by William d'Aubigny.

Norwich Castle: Founded by William the Conqueror sometime between 1066 and 1075.

Castle Rising Castle: Built in about 1138 by William d'Aubigny, 1st Earl of Arundel.

Weeting Castle: A fortified manor house built in the twelfth century.

Claxton Castle: Built in the fourteenth century but largely demolished to build Claxton Hall.

Baconsthorpe Castle: Built as a fortified manor house by William de la Pole in the fifteenth century.

Caister Castle: A fifteenth-century moated castle built by Sir John Fastolf between 1432 and 1446.

NORFOLK EXTRAVAGANCES

Thomas Howard, 3rd Duke of Norfolk, built his palace by the bank of the Wensum in Norwich between 1561 and 1563. This magnificent structure was said to be one of the finest town houses in England but in 1710 when the mayor of Norwich refused permission for the duke's company of comedians to enter the city with trumpets and due procession, the duke was outraged and immediately defaced his palace and ordered it to be demolished.

The magnificent Holkham Hall, constructed in the Palladian style for Thomas Coke, 1st Earl of Leicester, is estimated to have cost in the region of £90,000 (over £10 million in modern money). The construction nearly ruined the earl's heirs, rendering them unable to alter the house to suit changing tastes and consequently it has remained almost untouched since its completion in 1764.

Robert Walpole, Britain's first prime minister, set about enlarging his manor house at Houghton in 1722. He also desired a massive landscaped park to roll out before his house but the village of Houghton was not considered in keeping so he had it demolished and rebuilt it a mile further away.

George Walpole, 3rd Earl of Orford (1730–91), inherited Houghton Hall and its estates when he was just 21 years old. A genuine eccentric, a keen sportsman and profligate rake notable even in an age of aristocratic excess, he abandoned the family 'business' of politics, preferring to concentrate on field sports, horses and greyhounds – for the latter he established the rules of coursing. He enjoyed gambling but kept on losing to the degree that in 1778 he sold the art collection he had inherited to Catherine the Great of Russia for £40,000 to pay off his debts – and promptly named a greyhound 'Tzarina' to mark the occasion.

When John Hobart, 2nd Earl of Buckinghamshire and owner of Blickling Hall, died in 1793 he was buried in a pyramid erected upon the grounds of the hall.

The original 'secret millionaire' was James Webb; the man known simply as 'the benevolent stranger' visited Norwich and Yarmouth in February 1813 and distributed considerable sums of money among public institutions and needy poor.

In the early twentieth century, when the golden age of coaching was fading fast, Sir Thomas Cook of Sennowe Hall purchased a coach and a full livery to go with it. The Lobster Coach was established with a run carrying passengers between Cromer and Norwich with stops at St Faiths and Roughton. This 'gentleman's whimsy' also carried a cargo of fresh crabs and lobsters to grace the tables of the city's Maid's Head Inn.

The 6th Marquess of Cholmondeley started collecting model soldiers as a schoolboy. The fascination stayed with him and when he and his wife settled down in Houghton Hall in the 1950s he expanded and has one of the largest collections of model soldiers in the world.

TREASURES OF THE ANCIENTS FOUND ON OUR DOORSTEP

An earthen pot containing 500 pieces of ancient English silver coins including two gold angels of Henry VI, pennies from the Edwards and many groats of Henry VIII, was ploughed up in a field near Aylsham in March 1805.

An archaeological find of national importance was uncovered at Stow Heath, Felmingham, in 1844 when labourers were removing sand and a cave-in revealed two urns containing a hoard of religious bronzes with celestial symbolism from Roman, Celtic and oriental religion. Among the ritual material were found ceremonial staves, bronze ravens, a Celtic miniature wheel symbol and the hollow cast bronze head of the Roman god Jupiter, another of Minerva and a statuette of Lar with his drinking horn and cup. A couple of years later further finds were made nearby with the discovery of seventeen clay urns dating to the second century AD.

A golden torc ploughed up on Ken Hill at Snettisham in 1948 is described by the British Museum as 'the most famous object from Iron Age Britain' but it could have been lost forever. The ploughman who discovered it thought it was just an interesting lump of metal. He took it to the foreman and asked him what it was. The foreman declared it to be part of a brass bedstead and it lay for a week by the side of the field. More fragments of metal were drawn up and it was thanks to a rethink that the pieces were taken to Norwich Castle Museum where its antiquity and importance were recognised. The torc is skilfully crafted from sixty-four threads made from just over a kilogram of gold mixed with silver and is dated to the first half of the first century BC. It is one of the most elaborate golden objects made in the ancient world.

Further treasures were uncovered at Snettisham, notably in 1990 when a total of five hoards were found in the area. In one pit a nest of seven silver and bronze torcs were uncovered, but this was just a taste of things to come. Opening a larger pit two bronze bracelets were revealed, below them two silver torcs and then a prize of no less than ten gold torcs. The hoards contained a total of 175 torcs, seventy-five of them complete and fragments of about 100 more along with metal ingots and coins of the early, uninscribed variety, some of them early British types but the majority were Gallo-Belgic imports dated to about 70 BC.

The Thetford Treasure was discovered by a metal detectorist in 1979. Believed to have been buried in about AD 390 during a purge on religious cults, it contains such gems as a gold belt buckle, a duck-handled spoon, a small figure of Mercury, a key handle showing a lion eating a man and sets of blacksmith and farming tools. The British

Museum states the treasure is a find of national and international importance because it contains one of the finest sets of silver plate and jewellery known from the late Roman period.

SANDRINGHAM: THE COUNTRY RETREAT OF THE ROYALS

On 3 February 1862 HRH the Prince of Wales visited Norfolk to inspect the Sandringham Hall Estate 'with the view of purchasing it for shooting purposes, for which it is well adapted.' On 22 February it was announced that his Royal Highness had concluded the purchase for £220,000 and it was added by the *Norfolk Chronicle*: 'Norfolk people entertain strong hopes that they shall see a good deal of their future Sovereign.'

Wolferton station was the Royal Station serving Sandringham from its construction in 1862 until its closure in 1969. Among the royal visitors who passed over her platforms were: the King and Queen of Denmark (1893), King Carlos of Portugal (1895 and 1902), Queen Victoria (1899), the German Kaiser and his Empress (1899), the Dowager Empress of Russia (1907) and the King and Queen of Spain (1907).

The ornate platform lamps of Wolferton station are topped with miniature crowns.

The twenty-first birthday of Prince George (later George V) on 3 June 1886 saw a special royal train bring Sanger's Circus to Wolferton.

The German Kaiser and his Empress visited Sandringham between 25 and 28 November 1899. Accompanied by the Prince of Wales, they were met at Wolferton by the Princess of Wales, the Duke and Duchess of York and Princess Victoria of Wales. The Kaiser was reported as having been entertained, took part in a shoot and thoroughly enjoyed his visit.

King George V created his own private museum of big game trophies at Sandringham in 1928.

The Sandringham Estate had its own fire brigade; its magnificent 1939 Merryweather Fire Engine is on display in the estate museum.

Sandringham House is said to be haunted by a ghost who only makes his presence known at Christmas time.

A pigeon loft has been maintained on the Sandringham Estate since 1886.

Sugar, Heather and Susan, three of the Queen's corgis, are buried on the front lawn at Sandringham. Each one of them is marked by a small headstone carved with each pet's name, dates of their birth and death and the inscription 'The Faithful Companion of the Queen'.

Dig for Victory! During the Second World War some 1,433 acres were being farmed on the Sandringham Estate of which 977 were arable, 537 of which had been ploughed since the beginning of the war. This figure includes 6 acres of what was fine lawn in front of the house and a fine crop of oats and rye that was growing on what had been the golf course.

Fourteen members of the Women's Land Army were employed on the Sandringham Estate during the Second World War.

Queen Alexandra, her sons Prince Albert Victor, Duke of Clarence and Avondale, and George V, and grandson George VI, all died at Sandringham.

Prince John 'The Lost Prince' (12 July 1905–18 January 1919), the youngest son of King George V and Queen Mary, is buried in the churchyard of St Mary Magdalene Church, Sandringham.

The late Princess of Wales was born Diana Spencer on 1 July 1961 at Park House, Sandringham.

FIRE, FIRE!

Norwich, 4 May 1413: severe fire destroyed many properties including St Andrew's Hall and 25 April 1507; 700 houses destroyed. During the Baedeker Blitz of April 1942 extensive damage was caused by fire bombs across the city.

Reepham, 1543: Hackford Church destroyed and many houses on Back Street burnt to the ground.

Attleborough, 1559: The majority of the town destroyed.

East Dereham, 1 July 1581: The majority of the town destroyed and 27 January 1679 when 170 houses were burnt and property destroyed to the value of £19,500.

North Walsham, 25 June 1600: 118 houses, 70 shops, the Market Cross and many other buildings destroyed.

Wymondham, 11 June 1615: 300 properties destroyed including the town hall, school house and Market Cross.

Watton, 25 April 1673: 60 houses and shops destroyed to the value of £7,450.

Holt, 1 May 1708: The town was devastated by fire, the thatched roof of the chancel of the church destroyed and the lead melted in the windows. Damage was estimated to have been in the region of £11,000.

Fakenham, 4 August 1738: Serious damage was inflicted upon the town, with 26 houses destroyed.

Foulsham, 15 June 1770:
A massive fire destroyed both sides of the market place. 14 dwelling houses were destroyed and the church was reduced to a ruinous shell.

Swaffham, 19 November 1775: 24 houses burned down.

Great Yarmouth, 1941 and 1942: Large areas of the town including many of the old Rows and the historic Tolhouse and St Nicholas' Church were gutted during the bombing raids conducted upon the town by the Luftwaffe.

LOCATION, LOCATION, LOCATION: NORFOLK ON THE BIG SCREEN

The Silver Fleet starring Ralph Richardson and Googie Withers (1943): King's Lynn

The Wicked Lady starring Margaret Lockwood and James Mason (1945): Blickling Hall

The Dambusters starring Richard Todd and Michael Redgrave (1954): Langham airfield

Conflict of Wings starring John Gregson and Murial Pavlow (1954): Cley and Ludham

Barnacle Bill starring Alec Guinness (1957): Hunstanton pier

The Tomb of Ligeia film version of Edgar Allan Poe's ghost story directed by Roger Corman (1964): Castle Acre Priory

Operation Crossbow starring Sophia Loren (1965): Holkham Beach and Purfleet Street in King's Lynn

The Shuttered Room starring Gig Young, Carol Lynley and Oliver Reed (1967): Hardingham

The Witchfinder General starring Vincent Price and Ian Ogilvy (1968): St John's Church, Rushford near Thetford

The Go-Between starring Julie Christie and Alan Bates (1970): Filming centred around Melton Constable Hall but used many other locations in the county including Heydon, Thornage, Hickling Broad and Tombland in Norwich

Monty Python's *And Now for Something Completely Different* (1971): Near Norwich Castle and Elm Hill

Our Miss Fred, starring Danny la Rue (1974): Elm Hill, Norwich and other locations in the county

Julia, based on the novel *Pentimento* by Lilian Hellman, starring Jane Fonda and Vanessa Redgrave (1977): Winterton

Tarka the Otter (1979): Bintree Mill and Warham Salt Marshes

Memoirs of a Survivor starring Julie Christie and Nigel Hawthorne (1981): Argyle Street, Norwich

Out of Africa starring Robert Redford and Meryl Streep (1985): Castle Rising was turned into Denmark

Revolution starring Al Pacino, Nastassja Kinski and Donald Sutherland (1985): King's Lynn was transformed into eighteenth-century New York

Full Metal Jacket (1987): Set in Vietnam, but one scene involves a helicopter flying low over a paddy field firing its machine guns – it is actually flying over the Broads

The Grotesque starring Alan Bates and Sting (1995): Heydon Hall

Sense and Sensibility starring Emma Thompson, Hugh Grant and Kate Winslet (1995): Blickling Hall

Shakespeare in Love starring Gwyneth Paltrow and Joseph Fiennes (1998): Holkham beach

Eyes Wide Shut starring Tom Cruise and Nicole Kidman (1999): Thetford Forest

Wilt starring Griff Rhys Jones, Alison Steadman and Mel Smith (1990): Norwich, including Rose Lane car park (now demolished)

Die Another Day starring Pierce Brosnan as James Bond (2002): Turned farmland at Burnham Deepdale into a North Korean paddy field

A Cock and Bull Story, based on *Tristram Shandy* by Laurence Sterne starring Steve Coogan, Rob Brydon, Stephen Fry, Gillian Anderson and David Walliams (2004): Felbrigg, Blickling and Heydon Halls

The Last Hangman starring Timothy Spall (2005): West Raynham

Stardust starring Robert de Niro and Michelle Pfeiffer (2007): Elm Hill, Norwich

Atonement starring James McAvoy and Keira Knightley (2007): Walpole St Andrew

The Duchess starring Keira Knightley and Ralph Fiennes (2008): Holkham Hall and other locations along the North Norfolk coast including Cley Marshes

Scouting Book for Boys starring Holliday Grainger and Thomas Turgoose (2009): Holkham Bay, Great Yarmouth, Gresham Village, Broadland Sands Holiday Park

. . . AND THE SMALL SCREEN

Betjeman Goes By Train (1962): John Betjeman travelled the railway line from King's Lynn to Hunstanton via Wolferton and Snettisham

Weavers Green, Anglia Television soap opera starring Marjie Lawrence and Richard Coleman (1966): Heydon and other locations across the county

Dad's Army starring Arthur Lowe, John le Mesurier and Clive Dunn (1967–77) regularly used Thetford and its surrounding area for many of its external scenes such as Thetford Guildhall (Walmington-on-Sea Town Hall), Nether Row, the Bell Hotel, Palace Cinema and the Stanford Battle area. Other locations include Bardwell, Brandon, Bressingham, Honington, Oxburgh Hall, Santon Downham, Wacton, Wendling and the North Norfolk Railway

The Avengers episode 'The Town of No Return' starring Patrick Macnee and Diana Rigg (1965): Bircham Newton, Holkham Bay and Wighton

A Warning to the Curious written by Lawrence Gordon Clark, based on the M.R. James story of the same name (starring Peter Vaughan

and Clive Swift, BBC 1972): Filmed at Wells, Happisburgh, Holkham
and the North Norfolk Railway

Some Mothers Do 'Ave 'Em Christmas Special starring Michael
Crawford (1974): St Paul's and St Peter's Church Runham

The Nine Tailors, a Lord Peter Wimsey mystery starring Ian
Carmichael (1974): Walpole St Peter.

Danger UXB starring Anthony Andrews (1979) episode 'The Pier':
Cromer pier

'Allo 'Allo! starring Gorden Kaye, Carmen Silvera and Vicki Michelle
(1982–92): Thetford Forest, Lynford Hall, Denver Windmill, the
railway bridge at Briston, Beeston Church and the Muckleburgh
Collection, Weybourne

You Rang M'Lord (1988–93) starring Paul Shane and Su Pollard:
Lynford Hall, Oxburgh Hall, Diss and the North Norfolk Railway

The Sign of Four episode of *The Adventures of Sherlock Holmes*
starring Jeremy Brett (1987): Burgh Castle and Breydon Water. In
the same series *The Man with the Twisted Lip* was filmed at Up Hall,
Hillingdon

Tales of the Unexpected, now revered as a cult series, made by
Anglia TV (1979–88): Many Norfolk locations were used including
Oxburgh Hall ('The Vorpal Blade'), Lime Tree Farm, Thurning
('Royal Jelly'), Holt ('The Absence of Family'), Norwich Union's
Marble Hall ('Completely Foolproof'), Sennowe Park ('Poison'),
North Walsham ('The Moles'), Elm Hill ('Stranger in Town') and in
other episodes the locations include: Upper St Giles, Princes Street
and Bowthorpe Cemetery in Norwich, Thetford Forest, Hunstanton
Beach and Aylsham

The Chief, Anglia TV drama series with Tim Piggott-Smith then
Martin Shaw in the lead role (1990–5): Filmed across East Anglia
including Norwich, Great Yarmouth and Gorleston

Challenge Anneka starring Anneka Rice (1990) infamously repainted
Happisburgh Lighthouse but unfortunately the wrong type of paint
was used

Keeping Up Appearances episode 'Seaside Fun' starring Patricia Routledge and Clive Swift (1990): Great Yarmouth Pleasure Beach

Devices and Desires based on the book by P.D. James, starring Roy Marsden (1991): Featured a number of locations across the county including Cley Mill, Great Yarmouth, Holkham beach, Norwich Cathedral, Salthouse and Wells

Lovejoy starring Ian McShane (1986–94): mostly filmed in Suffolk but the series included a few locations in Norfolk and Norwich (Elm Hill)

September Song starring Russ Abbott and Michael Williams (1993–5): Cromer

Love on a Branch Line based on the novel by John Hadfield (1994): Oxburgh Hall, Heydon Hall, Lynford Hall and Sheringham and Weybourne stations on the North Norfolk Railway

Kavanagh QC starring John Thaw (1995): Norwich Cathedral

Dangerfield starring Nigel Le Valliant and Amanda Redmond (1995): Burnham Deepdale

The Mill on the Floss, based on the book by George Eliot starring Emily Watson and Bernard Hill (1997): Bintree Mill and Burgh-next-Aylsham

I'm Alan Partridge starring Steve Coogan (1997): includes scenes shot at Norwich railway station, Norwich Cathedral and the River Bure at Wroxham

Eastenders (1998): The popular soap filmed a special on the Norfolk Broads featuring Ludham Bridge Stores and locations at Horning

All the King's Men starring David Jason and Maggie Smith (1999): Sandringham, Wolferton station, Holkham Hall, Sheringham station, Cromer Pier, Blickling Hall and Burnham Deepdale

David Copperfield starring Bob Hoskins and Nicholas Lyndhurst (2000): King's Street, King's Lynn

The Lost Prince, directed by Stephen Poliakoff (2003): Holkham Hall and Weybourne station

Hitler's Britain, a documentary with reconstructions exploring what might have happened if Hitler had invaded in 1940 (2002): Heydon

Kingdom starring Stephen Fry, Celia Imrie and Hermione Norris (2007–9): Filming centred around Swaffham and Wells and used locations across the county including Happisburgh, Holkham beach, Dereham and Thetford

A SELECTION OF LESSER-KNOWN HISTORIC PLACES AND MUSEUMS

Caister St Edmund Roman Town, known to our ancestors as *Venta Icenorum*. Originally the civitas capital of the Iceni tribe, it became the Roman regional capital and served the surrounding area for trade, worship and entertainment after the occupation. Little remains above ground but the mounds and site are interpreted with information boards.

Cockley Cley Iceni Village includes farming and carriage museums, a seventeenth-century farmhouse with recreated interior and other exhibits of rural history. Probably not accurate to the satisfaction of purists, but a fun day out all the same.

Sainsbury Centre for Visual Arts on the UEA campus is open to all. Displays combine modern Western art with fine and applied arts from Africa, the Pacific, the Americas, Asia, Egypt, medieval Europe and the ancient Mediterranean, reflecting over 5,000 years of creativity. It is particularly well known for works by Henry Moore, Francis Bacon, John Davies and Alberto Giacometti.

Walsingham is known for its Shrine and Abbey Grounds but less known is the **Victorian Bridewell**. Erected in about 1787 it was enlarged and refitted as a County House of Correction in 1823. Frances Billing and Catherine Frarey, the notorious 'Burnham Poisoners' were held here. Closed in 1861, a two-storey wing remains today; it is unspoilt and very atmospheric.

Binham Priory was founded in the 1090s as a Benedictine priory and was the scene of a siege in the early thirteenth century. Legend tells of subterranean tunnels between Binham and Walsingham that are said to be haunted above and below ground by 'The Black Monk', possibly Alexander de Langley, once the Prior of Wymondham who went insane through too much study and was buried in chains here.

Creake Abbey was founded as an Augustinian Priory and elevated to the status of abbey in 1231. It was never a wealthy house and when fire swept through the buildings during the fourteenth century the funds were not available to rebuild it. In 1506 plague wiped out the remaining religious community, with the exception of the abbot. Today a few sections of church wall and foundation remain surrounded by farmland.

Fakenham Museum of Gas and Local History is the only surviving town gasworks in England and Wales that is still complete with all equipment used for the manufacture of gas. There are also displays of all manner of gas fittings and appliances once common to many homes.

The William Marriott Museum at the North Norfolk Railway's Holt station tells the story of the M&GN Railway and William Marriott, the man who engineered it. After looking around this fascinating museum, travel along a stretch of the M&GN on one of the steam trains that frequently runs throughout the summer.

The Shell Museum, Glandford, is the oldest purpose-built museum in Norfolk and houses the finest seashell collection in the United Kingdom.

The Norfolk Motorcycle Museum in Station Yard, North Walsham, is an interesting collection of over 80 motorcycles from the 1920s to the 1960s and provides a fascinating insight into the motorcycle industry of the past.

The Thursford Collection is a magical museum of mechanical organs, steam engines and fairground rides founded by George Cushing MBE. Robert Wolfe provides regular performances on the mighty Wurlitzer organ and between November and December the large exhibition hall is transformed into a theatre for the largest Christmas Spectacular show in England.

Strumpshaw Steam Museum, founded upon the collection of Mr Wesley Key, opened at its present location in 1954 and remains in family hands. The displays include mechanical organs and a narrow gauge railway but above all it is believed to be the largest private collection of steam engines in the country.

Stow Mill, Paston, was built in 1828 as a corn windmill. This picturesque mill has diagrams displayed on each of the four floors to explain how it once worked, along with an ever-growing collection of photographs and information to tell the mill's story through the years.

Cromer Museum has a fascinating display about the life and work of Cromer fisherfolk in the past as well as displays of local history, geology, fossils and Poppyland.

The RNLI Henry Blogg Museum at Cromer is a fine tribute to the greatest lifeboatman of all time and his crews. Inside are a wealth of items relating to the great man and his rescues, with the lifeboat *H.F. Bailey*, that served heroically under Blogg during the Second World War, as its centrepiece.

Swaffham Museum is housed in an eighteenth-century townhouse and contains fascinating local history displays reflecting centuries of history in the market town. There is also a special display gallery dedicated to Howard Carter and his discovery of the tomb of Tutankhamun in 1922.

Tales of the Old Gaol House at King's Lynn vividly brings to life the stories, punishments, sounds and smells of the old Lynn Gaol.

Wymondham Heritage Museum, in the town's historic bridewell, houses a rich array of local history including displays telling the stories of local heroes, rebels and villains.

The Museum of the Broads is the only waterside museum of Broadland life. Located in a traditional setting at Stalham Staithe on the Norfolk Broads, many of the boats once seen working or out for pleasure on the Broads are displayed along with the stories, tools and equipment of those who lived and worked in this unique area in the past.

The Dad's Army Museum, Thetford, is based in the town where the crews based themselves and filmed the exterior shots of Walmington-on-Sea in and around the area. The museum includes a nice selection of nostalgic items relating to the series and the Second World War.

Bishop Bonner's Cottage Museum at East Dereham is housed in a cottage that dates from 1502. Displays reflect a variety of aspects of the town's history and archaeology of the surrounding area.

The Mo Sheringham Museum is one of the newest in the county. It tells the story of the proud and independent people of Sheringham and is made all the more remarkable by its collection of the town's historic fleet of lifeboats.

A contender for Britain's smallest museum is **Mundesley Maritime Museum** housed in the old Mundesley Coastguard lookout building that dates back to 1928. Displays include an interesting array of photographs and artefacts from both the village's maritime and social past.

The City of Norwich Aviation Museum at Horsham St Faiths includes displays of aircraft and the history of military aviation in the county.

The 'Friendly Invasion' and sacrifice of USAAF servicemen and women in Norfolk is remembered at a number of airfield museums including: **The 100th Bomb Group Memorial Museum**, Thorpe Abbotts; **93rd Bomb Group Museum, Hardwick**; and **448th Bomb Group Museum**, Seething.

2

BATTLES & WARS

DISTANT DRUMS

King Henry I (King of England 1100–35) gave Banningham to Gerard Tusard. Afterwards it passed to Walter Tusard who held his serjeanty there and in Erpingham, by finding an archer on horseback with a crossbowman to attend the king whenever he made an expedition against the Welsh. This was on the proviso that he was to keep the archer and his horse in the king's army for forty days at his own cost.

In the south aisle within the Church of the Blessed Virgin Mary, Erpingham, is the monumental brass of Sir John de Erpingham in full armour who died on 1 August 1370. His son was Sir Thomas Erpingham who paid for the tower of the church to be erected. Both father and son were loyal, professional soldiers to their king. Sir Thomas is best remembered, and was even mentioned by Shakespeare in *Henry V*, for leading the British archers at the Battle of Agincourt on St Crispin's Day, 25 October 1415.

REBEL RISINGS

Peasants' Revolt, 1381

The Poll Tax was hitting hard and peasants rose up to protest at a number of places across England. In June 1381 Geoffrey 'John' Litster (also spelled Litester), a dyer of some means from Felmingham, led a rising in the north-eastern part of the county. Rebels also arrived in Thetford spreading revolt in the south-west of the county towards the Fens. Rebels converged on Norwich, Lynn and Swaffham. The main force in the county assembled on Mousehold Heath and marched on Norwich where they caused considerable damage to the property and possessions of poll tax collectors and officials, destroying legal records such as court rolls and taxation documents as they went. A further attack was made on Great Yarmouth.

Henry Despenser the 'Warlike Bishop' set off with his own retinue to engage the insurgents and gathered support from those who opposed the rebels as he marched across the county. Litster and his rebels fell back to North Walsham Heath where, on 25 or 26 June 1381, a bloody battle ensued. The rebels were no match for Despenser's better trained and equipped men. The denouement of the battle was the slaughter of the peasants who had fled to the unconsecrated footings of the new church in North Walsham after they mistakenly believed they might be able to claim sanctuary there. Litster was captured and hanged, drawn and quartered. His quarters were displayed at Norwich, Yarmouth, Lynn and his home near North Walsham as a stern warning to any other who would consider rebellion.

Gladman's Rising, 1443

The Abbot of St Benet at Holm was pressing for the removal of the new flour mills that had been built by the city on the Wensum and in January 1443 it appeared he would have his wish. City folks feared a shortage of flour and in an attempt to block the abbot's legal process, Robert Toppes, a former mayor, removed the common seal from the Guildhall. A full-scale riot, enflamed by old resentments over the power of the Church, ensued. Rioters led by such luminaries as the Mayor of Norwich, piled wood against the cathedral gates and threatened to burn the priory down.

In the midst of the riot it was arranged for John Gladman to ride into the city 'like a crowned king with a sceptre and sword carried before him.' Riding with him were twenty-four others 'with a crown upon their arms and carrying bows and arrows, as if they were valets of the crown of the lord king,' followed by a hundred more carrying bows and arrows and swords.They processed around the city and by the ringing of bells it was claimed they were able to gather 3,000 people and urged them 'to make a violent insurrection throughout the entire city . . . armed with swords, bows and arrows, hauberks and coats of armour.' The rioters held Norwich for a week, but once it was over indictments against the city trumped up their actions into a challenge against the king's authority. This was because Gladman's parade had been in mimicry of a royal procession and rioters were soon being branded in the documentation as 'rysers ageynst the kyng.'

The consequences of Gladman's Rising were serious for Norwich. The city was fined 3,000 marks (later reduced to 1,000), its liberties were seized by the king and Sir John Clifton of New Buckenham was imposed upon the city to rule it as governor for four years.

Kett's Rebellion, 1549

On 6 July 1549 the feast of the translation of St Thomas á Becket was celebrated at Wymondham. Recent enclosures of land around the town acted as a catalyst for local folk to rise up and start smashing down fences at Hethersett. When the mob arrived at Robert Kett's enclosures he joined them and helped tear down his own fences.

The rioters mustered again in Wymondham on 8 July and marched on Norwich with Robert Kett at their head. Refused entry by the city, the rebel force made camp upon Mousehold, established a council headed by Kett who sat under the 'Oak of Reformation', and drew up a charter of demands righting the wrongs done to commoners. A royal herald came to Kett's Camp and offered a pardon but Kett refused saying they had offended no laws and did not require one, only for a boy to then step forward and defecate in front of the herald to show his contempt. The herald went away denouncing Kett as a traitor. The following day the rebels stormed the city.

A royal army under the Marquess of Northampton arrived at Norwich on 31 July. The rebels fell back but returned again the same night, and the fighting continued to the early hours resulting in many deaths including Lord Sheffield. A considerably larger force of 14,000 men under the Earl of Warwick arrived at the city on 23 August. Another herald offered Kett a pardon but was again rejected. Three days of intense fighting then commenced with the final battle fought upon Dussin's Dale. 3,000 rebels were slain, the rebellion was put down and many of the surviving rebels were publicly hanged as a warning to others.

The worst fate awaited the Kett brothers. Robert was paraded through Norwich and brought to the foot of the castle where a rope was fixed about his neck. He was drawn up to a gibbet upon the battlements and left hanging there until his body wasted away, and similar was done to his brother William at Wymondham.

The Norwich Conspiracy, 1570

The great 'Stranger' immigration of 1567 brought a substantial Flemish and Walloon community of Protestant weavers to the City of Norwich to pass on their skills. In the main they seem to have been welcomed but there were dissenting voices. George Redman of Cringleford spoke out against the 'Strangers' claiming they were taking the jobs and livelihood of the citizens of Norwich and demanded that they should be sent home and if they were not he threatened to 'string up the Sheriff' and 'levy a force'. Joined by gentlemen John Throgmorton, John Appleyard the Sheriff of Norwich and Thomas Brooke of Rollesby, they formed two groups with Redman raising a force in Cringleford and another being levied at Harleston Fair. Magistrates were informed of these actions; John Throgmorton was first to be apprehended followed by a number of others and the rising was put down before it really got started and the three ring leaders suffered the dreadful fate of being hanged, drawn and quartered.

ARMADA DEFENCES

During the Spanish Armada scare of 1588 the fortifications of Yarmouth were put into a state of readiness; a boom was thrown across the Haven at the South Gates and a mound of earth was raised higher than the walls. Called the South Mount, it had several pieces of ordnance placed upon it. Another mound, known as the New Mount, was afterwards thrown up near St George's Chapel, and preparations were made to lodge and provision a garrison of 1,000 men and a war-like ship was fitted out at the town's expense 'to annoy the enemy at sea'. It is also worthy of note that King's Lynn contributed five ships to the fleet which sailed against the Spanish Armada.

Skilled military engineer Captain York drew up ambitious plans for the defence of Norfolk. Along the coast he suggested the enlargement of the earth fortification at Weybourne, the construction of a new fort at Cley Haven and a rampart between the two. Further defences were planned at Great Yarmouth, Acle, Potter Heigham, Wroxham and Wayford Bridge to prevent penetrations by the enemy as well as a reconsideration of the defences of Norwich. However, little of this was carried out as the danger from the Armada had passed before considerable works could be undertaken.

THE CIVIL WAR

Norfolk officially sided with Parliament during the Civil War, and though no great battles were fought here . . .

Local landowner Hamon L'Estrange held King's Lynn for the king against a siege by Parliamentary forces in 1643. Lynn had shakily declared for Parliament but L'Estrange, a Royalist sympathiser, was appointed governor. He struck a deal with Charles I, whereby if Lynn declared for the crown the king would send troops. On 28 August 1643 the town closed its doors to an attacking force of some 18,000 Parliamentarian soldiers under the command of the Earl of Manchester. The town was prepared for the siege with 500 barrels of gunpowder in store and about forty guns mounted on the ramparts. The ensuing weeks of bombardment caused severe damage to defences and dwellings in the town, even St Margaret's Church was blasted during a sermon with a 16lb shot which shattered a pillar and showered parishioners in stained glass. The casualties incurred during the Siege of Lynn were minimal – figures of up to eighty deaths are quoted. The Royalist forces within the walls of Lynn were never to be relieved . . . the Earl of Warwick made sure of that when he blockaded The Wash with his squadron of warships. Growing weak through lack of food and with no hope of relief, the garrison were finally forced to ask for terms after the besiegers paraded in full strength before the walls of the town. Lynn opened its gates on 16 September and the Earl of Manchester's army marched in to occupy for Parliament.

On Monday 24 April 1648 crowds of those loyal to Charles I rose up in Norwich and stormed the headquarters of the County Committee, not far from St Peter Mancroft Church on what is now known as Bethel Street. When Parliamentarian cavalry arrived to put down the uprising, fierce fighting broke out and more arms were looted from the Committee House. But in their haste to break open some gunpowder casks and carry off the contents, rioters had spilt large quantities of it through the building. It ignited and exploded some ninety barrels of gunpowder. To give an idea of the scale of this blast, Guy Fawkes and his conspirators planned to use thirty-six barrels of gunpowder to blow up the Houses of Parliament. What became known as 'The Great Blowe' is believed to have been the largest explosion during the English Civil War. Forty rioters were killed, over 120 were injured by the blast and it devastated the immediate vicinity of the explosion. It blew out the windows of St Peter Mancroft and St Stephen's churches and sent timbers, tiles, wood, plaster, stone and lead debris and bits of victims showering down across the city.

IN THE EVENT OF INVASION – NAPOLEONIC STYLE

During the invasion scare of the early nineteenth century, the brass ordnance of Norwich City was tested by locally stationed artillerymen. Four of these guns burst, but the old iron nine-pounders stood the test. A brass gun used during Kett's Rebellion in 1549 was preserved as a relic.

At a meeting of the deputy lieutenants and magistrates of Norfolk in June 1803, presided over by the Marquess Townshend, a system of communication and a scheme of general defence and preservation of property in the county, in the event of an invasion, were agreed. The county was then formed into thirteen divisions. Each division was placed under the charge of a lieutenant nominated by the Lord Lieutenant and each Hundred in the various divisions was placed under a magistrate, to be known as an Inspector of the Hundred.

Each parish was under a gentleman, clergyman or principal farmer, and he was termed Superintendent of the Parish.

Telegraphs, flags or tar barrels were all used on top of church towers and some of the principal residences in the county were to create a chain of communication by day or night in the event of enemy landings during the Napoleonic Wars. Bonfires were also prohibited at this time, lest they cause a false alarm. The telegraph system could work surprisingly well; in 1807 it was recorded that an order from the Admiralty Office in London was received at Yarmouth just 17 minutes later.

The first parade of the Norwich Regiment of Volunteer Infantry took place on 1 September 1803. The new unit consisted of eight battalion companies, a light infantry and a grenadier company. At the end of their parade, the members of the corps drew from five barrels of British stout and drank to the king's health, the prosperity of their country and city, and success to the corps.

The Great Yarmouth Southtown Armoury was built in 1806 by Mr Wyatt at a cost of £15,000. During the war some 10,000 stand of arms were held within it.

In 1804 the ladies of Lynn inaugurated a movement for making flannel underclothing for the use of the men of the Lynn Volunteers.

The first battle drill of the new Norfolk Volunteer Corps was staged with locally based artillery and Shropshire Militia at Bramerton Common on 18 October 1803. General Milner commended all arms for their steadiness on parade.

In December 1803 the twenty-two units of Yeomanry Cavalry raised in the county were formed into three regiments. Marquess Townshend was appointed Colonel of the Western Regiment; Major-General Money, the Colonel of the Eastern Regiment and Colonel Bulwer was made Colonel of the Mid-Norfolk Regiment.

The Old Buckenham Volunteers consisted of five officers and 125 non-commissioned officers and men.

In January 1804 Private John Baker of the Loddon Volunteers was dismissed for refusing to take the oath of allegiance to His Majesty.

Consequently Baker was 'subjected to every ignominy' in front of the troops whereby, 'His arms and accoutrements, together with the Volunteer clothing, were stripped off on parade, much to the satisfaction of the whole corps.'

On 4 February 1804, as the Cromer Sea Fencibles were taking part in a canister and grape shot practice on the beach, a ball struck Captain Temlett RN on the foot and another shattered the leg of John Smith to the degree that an immediate amputation was required. A public subscription, amounting to £500 was made for Mr Smith.

On 23 July 1807 an impressive fleet of twenty-four sail of the line assembled in the Yarmouth Roads under the command of Admiral James Gambier ready to sail for the Baltic (they saw action in the Second Battle of Copenhagen).

In 1810 a young woman from Dereham, being strongly attached to a soldier of the 24th Regiment, resolved to follow him to the wars. Dressing in male attire she went to Norwich but enlisted in the 54th Regiment by mistake. Her true gender was discovered, her plans frustrated and the event became the subject of a popular ballad.

After the Battle of Waterloo in 1815, 600 of the returned wounded were lodged at the Great Yarmouth Naval Hospital.

THE THREE ADMIRALS OF COCKTHORPE

Norfolk has a long and noble naval tradition but no other village in our county can claim such strong links with no less than three distinguished admirals. The first connection is a little tenuous; Sir Christopher Myngs (1635–66) was a native of Salthouse but is said to have spent some of his formative years at Cockthorpe. Sir John Narborough was christened at Cockthorpe on 11 October 1640; present at the Battle of Lowestoft and at Sole Bay, he distinguished himself fighting against the Barbary Coast pirates. Cloudesley Shovell was a descendant of Myngs; he was christened at Cockthorpe on 25 November 1650 and served in many of the significant naval actions of the late seventeenth and early eighteenth centuries, rising to become Commander-in-Chief of the British fleet and a national hero.

SOME BITS ABOUT NELSON

Admiral Horatio Nelson was Britain's greatest naval commander of all time. Truly a son of Norfolk, he was to say 'I am myself a Norfolk man and glory in being so.'

Nelson was born at Burnham Thorpe Rectory on 29 September 1758, the sixth of eleven children of the Revd Edmund and Catherine Nelson and learned to sail from an early age on the creeks, broads and sea around North Norfolk.

Nelson attended King Edward VI's Grammar School in Norwich and the Paston School, North Walsham. He joined his first ship directly from the latter school on 1 January 1771 aged twelve, reporting to HMS *Raisonnable* as an ordinary seaman and coxswain under his maternal uncle, Captain Maurice Suckling, who commanded the vessel.

Nelson suffered dreadful seasickness.

He lost his right arm when fighting at Santa Cruz in Tenerife in July 1797. He received a musket ball shot just above his right elbow and the ship's surgeon had no option but to amputate the forearm.

During the Battle of the Nile (Aboukir Bay) in Egypt on 1 August 1798, Nelson was hit above his right eye by a fragment of shot. Bleeding profusely, pale and concussed, he carried on with the battle. Nelson did not lose his eye but lost his sight in it and he suffered from sporadic blinding headaches caused by this injury for the rest of his life.

An annual Venison Feast was held at the Red Lion, Fakenham, to celebrate Lord Nelson's victory at the Battle of the Nile.

National hero, Vice Admiral Nelson visited Great Yarmouth on 6 November 1800. Greeted with much enthusiastic acclaim and given the Freedom of the Borough, during the ceremony he was asked to place a hand on the Bible, the flustered town clerk, who had not noticed Nelson's amputation blurted out; 'Your right hand, my Lord,' to which the Admiral gave the withering reply: 'That is at Tenerife.' Later in the day when the landlady of the Wrestler's Arms asked him if she might change the inn's name to the Nelson's Arms, he delightedly told her that the name would be absurd as he only had one.

A magnificent portrait of Admiral Nelson by Sir William Beechey was placed in St Andrew's Hall, Norwich in 1799 and is still on display at Blackfriar's Hall to this day.

The sword of the Spanish Admiral Don Xavier Francisco Winthuysen, who surrendered to Nelson before he died of his wounds at the Battle of St Vincent on 14 February 1797, was presented to the City of Norwich by Lord Nelson and placed in a mural monument at the Guildhall.

Nelson's grasp of strategy produced a number of decisive victories and he was noted for his ability to inspire and bring out the best in his men, a skill which became known simply as the 'Nelson touch'.

During the Battle of Copenhagen on 2 April 1801, when the flag signals were raised ordering a withdrawal, Nelson turned to Foley, his flag captain, and said: 'You know, Foley, I have only one eye. I have a right to be blind sometimes.' He then put his telescope to his blind eye, and said 'I really do not see the Signal!' and fought on to victory.

Nelson sustained his final and fatal wound at about 1.00 p.m. on 21 October 1805 during the Battle of Trafalgar. He was shot through the shoulder and spine by a French sniper and stated: 'I have but a short time to live; my back is shot through.' He was carried below decks and died at approximately 4.30 p.m.

His body was placed in a cask of brandy mixed with camphor and myrrh, which was then lashed to the *Victory*'s mainmast and put under guard. It led to the phrase 'tapping the Admiral' when sailors had a tot of rum.

Nelson's state funeral took place on 9 January 1806. His funeral procession consisted of thirty-two admirals, over 100 captains and an escort of 10,000 troops, which took the coffin from the Admiralty to

St Paul's Cathedral, London. After a four-hour service he was laid to rest within a sarcophagus originally carved for Cardinal Wolsey.

Norfolk paid its own homage to Nelson by erecting the first 'Nelson's Column' on the South Denes at Great Yarmouth. The first stone was laid in August 1817 and it was finally completed in 1819. Paid for by nearly £7,000 in subscriptions, it predated the Trafalgar Square column by over twenty years. The column is topped not by Nelson, but by Britannia, who stands gazing towards the north-west, and Burnham Thorpe, the birthplace of Nelson.

TEN FACTS ABOUT THE ROYAL NORFOLK REGIMENT

The regiment was one of five raised in 1685 during the Monmouth Rebellion. It was originally known as Colonel Henry Cornwall's Regiment and was designated the 9th Regiment of Foot in 1751.

The figure of Britannia was bestowed upon the regiment by Queen Anne in recognition of the bravery, steadfastness and example of its men at the Battle of Almanza in 1707.

During the evacuation of the beach during the Battle of Corunna on 16 January 1809, the regiment had provided the rearguard. Their final act before leaving was to bury the body of their Divisional Commander Sir John Moore. Ever since that time details of black featured on the uniform of the regiment in memory of Sir John.

During the First Sikh War the regiment marched 150 miles in six days and then fought the Battle of Ferozeshah on 21/22 December 1845.

The colours of the Norfolk Regiment were last carried in action during the Second Afghan War (1878–80).

The original regimental march was 'Young May Moon' until 1880 when 'Rule Britannia' by Dr Thomas Augustine Arne was adopted.

The 9th or East Norfolk Regiment was given its new official title of the Norfolk Regiment in the Cardwell Reforms (Childers Reforms) of 1881.

Britannia Barracks was built between 1886 and 1887 by Norwich City Council and presented to the Norfolk Regiment as its first permanent depot.

The Norfolk Regiment was created the Royal Norfolk Regiment in Army Order 110, on the occasion of the Silver Jubilee of HM King George V in 1935 which coincided with the 250th anniversary of the regiment.

The Royal Norfolk Regiment was amalgamated with the Suffolk Regiment to form the 1st Battalion, the East Anglian Regiment in 1959. A further amalgamation with other East Anglian regiments occurred in 1964 creating the Royal Anglian Regiment. Today, the successor to the 9th Foot is 'A' Company, 1st Battalion, the Royal Anglian Regiment

THE HOLY BOYS

Contrary to some stories that tell of our Norfolk Regiment soldiers selling Bibles for beer, the nickname of the Holy Boys actually came from the Regiment's time in Spain and Portugal during the Peninsular War (1807–14). At this time the figure of Britannia that was emblazoned large upon the regimental colours and badges was mistaken by locals in the Catholic countries for the Virgin Mary, and the entire regiment was believed to be made up of 'holy men'.

FIRST LONG SERVICE?

The earliest known example of a long service medal to the 9th Foot is believed to be a large hallmarked silver medallion presented to Joseph Scott by the officers of the IX or East Norfolk Regiment on the completion of his tenth year as their Quartermaster in 1817.

SOLDIERS OF THE QUEEN

The first Norfolk man to receive the Victoria Cross was Pte Henry Ward who was born at Harleston in 1823. During the Indian Mutiny, Ward was a member of the 78th Regiment of Foot (later the Seaforth Highlanders) and gained his award for saving the life of

Captain Henry Havelock and his dooly while under heavy crossfire at Lucknow on the night of 25/26 September 1857. Ward later achieved the rank of Quartermaster Sergeant, while Henry Havelock became a Major General and retained Ward as his personal servant. Today, Ward's VC is displayed at the Regimental Museum of the Queen's Own Highlanders in Fort George, Invernesshire, Scotland.

William Goate was born at Fritton on 12 January 1836 and by the age of twenty-two was a Lance Corporal in the 9th Lancers. During

the Indian Mutiny, at Lucknow on 6 March 1858, Goate saw that Major Smyth, an officer of 2nd Dragoon Guards, had been wounded. He immediately dismounted in the presence of a number of the enemy and attempted to remove the wounded officer to safety but, being surrounded by the enemy cavalry, Goate had to relinquish his attempt, though he went a second time under a heavy fire to recover the body. Recognised for his indefatigable bravery, William Goate was awarded the VC and was later promoted to corporal.

The Revd James William Adams, rector of Postwick, Stow Bardolph and Wimbotsham, had been a chaplain in the Bengal Ecclesiastical Department and was serving as chaplain to the Kabul Field Force during the Second Afghan War. During the action at Killa Kazi on 11 December 1879, some men of the 9th Lancers having fallen (with their horses) into a wide and deep 'nullah' or ditch, and the enemy being close upon them, the Revd Adams rushed into the water-filled ditch, dragged the horses from off the men and extricated the troopers under a heavy fire and with the enemy closing in. Adams had let go of his horse in order to render more effectual assistance and had to escape on foot. This remarkably brave chaplain was awarded the VC for his gallant actions.

Padre George Smith was born at Docking on 8 January 1845, the son of the local shoemaker. Despite his humble beginnings he went on to study theology at St Augustine's College, Canterbury, and proceeded to Natal as a missionary in 1871. When the Zulu War broke out in

1877 Smith was attached to the British Army as an assistant army chaplain and was at the mission station of Rorke's Drift on 22/23 January 1879 when it was attacked by a force of some 3,000–4,000 Zulu warriors. Although as a chaplain he was a non-combatant, Smith was highly commended for his bravery in the defence as he distributed ammunition to the soldiers of the 24th Regiment of Foot who were manning the barricades. In light of his deeds in the action, Smith was offered an appointment as a regular army chaplain and served for many years after on campaign in Egypt and the Sudan – but the legacy of Rorke's Drift stayed with him in his nickname of 'Ammunition Smith'.

William Mordaunt Marsh Edwards, the son and heir of Henry Bartholomew of Hardingham Hall, was a twenty-seven-year-old lieutenant serving in the 2nd Battalion, the Highland Light Infantry when on 13 September 1882 during the Battle of Tel-el-Kebir, Egypt, he led a party of his men to storm a redoubt. Leading from the front, he rushed alone into the battery, killed the artillery officer in charge and was himself knocked down by a gunner with a rammer and was rescued only by the timely arrival of three men of his regiment. His bravery and example were recognised by the award of the Victoria Cross. Edwards was later promoted to major and was honoured in Norfolk by being made a Deputy Lieutenant. He died in 1912 and was buried in St George's Churchyard at Hardingham.

The names of Norfolk men published among the list of those who had distinguished themselves at the Battle of El Teb (4 February 1884 and 29 February 1884) include: Colonel Sir Redvers Buller of Castle Rising; Commander Rolfe of Heacham; Major Haggard, son of Mr Haggard of East Braddenham, and Naval Captain Arthur Knyvett Wilson of Swaffham who was awarded the VC for his bravery in this action.

Stephen Weller, as colonel's trumpeter in the 16th Lancers, sounded the charge of the regiment at the Battle of Aliwal on 28 January 1846. Living out his last years in Norfolk, he died in the Norfolk & Norwich Hospital on 10 November 1881.

Lieutenant-Colonel Horace Stopford, killed in action commanding the 2nd Battalion the Coldstream Guards at the Battle of Modder River on 28 November 1899, had been a resident of Sheringham and Captain of the Sheringham Golf Club in 1895.

Major Bernard Leathes Prior, the man who helped to established and later commanded the Norfolk Volunteer Infantry Brigade Cyclists, published one of the first training manuals for bicycle-mounted soldiers entitled *The Military Cyclist: Notes on the Work of the Individual Soldier* in 1907.

John David Francis Shaul was born at King's Lynn on 11 September 1873. Serving as a corporal in the 1st Battalion, the Highland Light Infantry during the Second Boer War, during the Battle of Magersfontein on 11 December 1899, Shaul was in charge of stretcher-bearers, his citation states:

> He was most conspicuous during the day in dressing men's wounds, and in one case he came, under a heavy fire, to a man who was lying wounded in the back and with the utmost; coolness and deliberation, sat down beside the wounded man and proceeded to dress his wound. Having done this, he got up and went quietly to another part of the field. This act of gallantry was performed under a continuous and heavy fire as coolly and quietly as if there had been no enemy near.

Corporal John Shaul was the last Norfolk man to receive the Victoria Cross during the reign of Queen Victoria.

THE GREAT MANOEUVRES – OR – THE LAST INVASION OF NORFOLK

British Army manoeuvres of an unprecedented scale were conducted across East Anglia in 1912. The forces were nearly equal in size; the Staff of the Red Army under General Haig were Aldershot command, who were accustomed to working together. In contrast, the Blue Army under General Grierson were drawn from all commands except Aldershot with two brigades drawn from Household Cavalry, Scots Greys, Yeomanry and Cyclists. The Blue infantry came from the Southern Command (3rd Division), Eastern Command (4th Division) and the Territorial Force. The main concentration of troops in Norfolk was in Swaffham with over 2,000 Red troops predominantly from 2nd and 3rd Grenadier Guards and 2nd Coldstream Guards. All ranks and services included, the total number of troops involved

A WORLD OF SHAMS

OFFICER (*of Umpire Staff*). "Hi, you there! You mustn't cross here! Can't you see the notice? This bridge is supposed to be destroyed." SUBALTERN (*cheerfully*). "Oh, that's all right! We're supposed to be swimming across."

across East Anglia amounted to nearly 50,000. The scenario was that the Blue army invaded and the Red army defended. Blues won.

During the manoeuvres it was soon painfully apparent that Haig had not realised the importance of the spotter aircraft. Grierson, the victorious commander of the Blue army, had hidden his troops from observation and Haig had failed to ascertain their movements or deployment. In contrast, Grierson had used his spotters well and had almost perfect knowledge of the movements of Haig's troops. In the final analysis of the manoeuvres, in spite of the efforts of the umpires and judges to make the contest appear more even, Haig was simply out-generalled by Grierson.

THE FIRST WORLD WAR

Fears of invasion by Germans in East Anglia were stirred up from 1906 when William Le Queux published *The Invasion of 1910*. The book takes the form of a military history where the Germans land a sizeable invasion force on the East Coast of England. It includes excerpts from the characters' journals and letters and descriptions of the fictional

German campaign itself that give it an eerie sense of realism. The fear was further fuelled by Le Queux in *Spies of the Kaiser* (1909) which featured much of Norfolk, including enemy spies at work in Weybourne, Kelling and Sheringham and a pursuit of enemy agents by motor car through Wymondham to the Norfolk coast, featuring such places as Aylsham, North Walsham, Witton, Paston and Cromer.

Winston Churchill, as First Lord of the Admiralty, instigated the first moves to mobilise the British Fleet onto a war footing from the Sea Marge Hotel at Overstrand in July 1914. His holiday home, Pear Tree Cottage, was only a short distance away but it was not equipped with a telephone.

The first battalion of the Norfolk Regiment to occupy their war station were 6th (Cyclist) Battalion, a Territorial Force unit whose duty was to provide anti-invasion patrols along the North Norfolk coast from Wells to Gorleston. They established their headquarters at the Council School, Manor Road, North Walsham on 5 August 1915.

The first experience of offensive enemy action upon the county during the First World War occurred at about 7.00 a.m. on the misty morning of Tuesday 3 November 1914, when Great Yarmouth was shelled from the sea by battleships of the German Navy. The misty weather conditions meant the bombardment was ineffective and the shells fell short of any target, the majority of their shrapnel landing on the beach at Gorleston.

The First World War 'pillbox' defences in Bradfield and along the River Ant as defensive points in the event of an invasion are some of the first of their kind ever built.

During the First World War there were spy scares across the country but they were particularly acute in Norfolk. German waiters arrested by troops at Cromer under the Defence of the Realm Act in 1914 were displayed in Norwich Market Place as German spies.

One of just two armoured trains in the country was based in Norfolk. Consisting of four armoured wagons and armed with two 12-pounder guns and two machines guns it ran along the M&GN branch line to Mundesley with occasional trips as far afield as Yarmouth and Lowestoft.

The first bombs dropped by a Zeppelin in an air raid over Great Britain fell upon Norfolk on 19 January 1915. The attack was carried out by two Zeppelin raiders, the L3 under Kapitänleutnant Hans Fritz and L4 under the command of Kapitänleutnant Magnus Count von Platen Hallermand. Both airships made landfall near Bacton, L4 turned to follow the coastline towards the west while L3 turned south-east. The L3 dropped its first bomb, an incendiary, on farmer George Humphrey's waterlogged paddocks near St Michael's Church at Little Ormesby, leaving only a small crater about 18in wide. The first bomb to hit a building was dropped by Zeppelin L4 and fell on Whitehall Yard, Windham Street, Sheringham. During the attack the two Zeppelin raiders dropped bombs on Snettisham, Heacham, Hunstanton, Great Yarmouth and King's Lynn, where in these latter named places a total of four people were killed and many more were wounded.

After the Zeppelin raid of 19 January 1915 a number of people gave statements to the press that the aerial raiders had been guided to their targets by the powerful headlamps of a mystery car. Such was the concern, King's Lynn MP Holcombe Ingleby collected together the testimony of witnesses, published a booklet entitled 'The Zeppelin Raid in West Norfolk' and even asked questions about the matter in Parliament.

The last Zeppelin to be shot down in Britain during the First World War, the L70, was brought down by Major Egbert Cadbury and Captain Robert Leckie flying a DH-4 from the Royal Naval Air Service base at Great Yarmouth on 5 August 1918. The L70 came down about 8 miles just north of Wells-next-the-Sea, close to the schooner *Amethyst*. A search of the sea soon revealed none of the crew had survived.

It is recorded and attested that the last British soldier to leave the shores of Gallipoli during the evacuation of 20 December 1915 was Sergeant Robert Pymar of the King's Own Royal Regiment, Norfolk Yeomanry.

Edith Cavell, the greatest British heroine of the First World War, was born the daughter of the rector of Swardeston on 4 December 1865. While working as the Matron of the École Belge d'Infirmières Diplômées at Brussels she was arrested by the German invaders and tried for 'conducting soldiers to the enemy'. Found guilty, she was shot by a German firing squad at the Tir Nationale (National Rifle Range) on 12 October 1915. After the war her body was exhumed and returned for burial at Life's Green, at the east side of Norwich Cathedral, on 19 May 1919.

High on the cliffs of Hunstanton stood the Hippisley Hut. Named after the commanding officer of the establishment Lieutenant-Commander Richard John Bayntun Hippisley, the hut and the cliffs immediately around it were kept sealed off. The purpose of the hut's activities were maintained as top secret during the war for this little building housed, what was in its day, the very latest receivers to listen in to the transmissions of enemy shipping or aircraft. The German Navy were confident they could not be heard and never made any attempt to conceal their wireless traffic.

The last serious air raid conducted by a Zeppelin over Norfolk occurred shortly before 9.00 p.m. on Wednesday 9 September 1915 when Zeppelin L14, under the command of Kapitänleutnant Alois Böcker, dropped a number of bombs on East Dereham causing serious damage around the Church Street area, killing three and fatally injuring two soldiers.

At 10.55 p.m. on Monday 14 January 1918, Great Yarmouth was shelled by German warships for the last time. Some shells did hit their mark – houses and buildings were damaged, windows were blown in, eight people were injured and four killed.

TANKS!

The first British tanks were were put through their paces in a secret training area on Lord Iveagh's estate on the Norfolk and Suffolk borders at Elvedon near Thetford. To ensure no prying eyes could see, long hoardings covered in hessian were put along the boundaries of the estate near public roads, the excuse being these were to protect passing traffic from gun shell explosions. When these landships were finally removed to the front line, their secret was maintained by any reference in their shipment being referred to as 'tanks', as in water tanks, and the name stuck.

WE MADE IT . . .

Howlett & White Ltd, just one of a number of large-scale boot and shoemaking businesses in Norwich made 453,000 pairs of boots and shoes for the British Army: 32,000 for the Allies and 21,000 British Aviation Boots during the First World War.

Norwich engineering firm Boulton & Paul Ltd went into aircraft production and made 2,530 aircraft (notably the FE.2b, Sopwith Camel and Snipe) and 7,835 propellers in their Norwich factories.

Barnards Ltd Engineers produced over 6,994 miles of wire netting for the War Office and Admiralty.

THE VANISHED BATTALION?

On 12 August 1915 the 5th Battalion, the Norfolk Regiment sustained heavy casualties during an attack at Kuchuk Anafarta Ova on the Gallipoli peninsula. The fighting had extended into the enemy lines and not knowing if the men had been killed or taken prisoner, many families were simply notified that their relative was 'Missing'. The battalion contained a company of men from the Sandringham estate and King George V took a personal interest in their fate, pressing for information, but specifics could not be given. Sir Ian Hamilton's despatch describes 'a very mysterious thing' where 'the colonel, sixteen officers and 250 men, still kept pushing on, driving the enemy before them . . . Nothing more was ever seen or heard of any of them. They charged into a forest and were lost to sight or sound. Not one of them ever came back.' The bodies of the 5th Battalion soldiers who fell on that day were discovered by the Graves Registration Unit in September 1919. Sadly most were beyond individual identification but the damage was done and the 'mystery' of the disappearing Norfolks had entered into military myth. It has been discussed in serious and scurrilous publications ever since.

THE ONLY NORFOLK REGIMENT FIRST WORLD WAR VC

The only member of the Norfolk Regiment to be awarded the Victoria Cross in the First World War was John Sherwood-Kelly, an Acting Lieutenant-Colonel of the Norfolk Regiment, on detachment Commanding 1st Battalion, the Royal Inniskilling Fusiliers. On 20 November 1917 at Marcoing, France, when a party of men were held upon the near side of a canal by heavy rifle fire, Sherwood-Kelly at once ordered covering fire, personally led his company across the canal and then reconnoitred, under heavy fire, the high ground held by the enemy. He took a Lewis gun team, forced his way through obstacles and covered the advance of his battalion, enabling them to capture the position. Later he led a charge against some pits from which heavy fire was coming, capturing five machine guns and forty-six prisoners.

MOST DECORATED

Norfolk's most highly decorated soldier of the First World War was Sergeant Harry Cator VC, MM, Croix de Guerre. Born on 24 January 1884 the son of a railway worker at Drayton, he was educated at Drayton School. Harry married on 2 September 1914, enlisted the following day and proceeded to France with 7th Battalion, the East Surrey Regiment on 23 June 1915. He received his first award, the Military Medal for Gallantry in the Field in 1916 during the Battle of the Somme for helping to rescue thirty-six men who had become tangled in enemy barbed wire in no man's land – he was also decorated with France's Croix de Guerre avec Palme. Harry's VC was awarded for action at Hangest Trench during the Battle of Arras on 19 April 1917. His citation states the award was:

> For most conspicuous bravery and devotion to duty. Whilst consolidating the first line captured system his platoon suffered severe casualties from hostile machine-gun and rifle fire. In full view of the enemy and under heavy fire Sergeant Cator, with one man, advanced to attack the hostile machine gun. The man accompanying him was killed after going a short distance, but Sergeant Cator continued on and picking up a Lewis gun and some

drums on his way succeeded in reaching the northern end of the hostile trench. Meanwhile, one of our bombing parties was seen to be held up by a machine gun. Sergeant Cator took up a position from which he sighted this gun and killed the entire team and the officer whose papers he brought in. He continued to hold that end of the trench with the Lewis gun and with such effect that the bombing squad was enabled to work along, the result being that one hundred prisoners and five machine guns were captured.

Three days later he was severely wounded by a bursting shell that shattered his jaw. He recovered from his wounds and was presented with his VC personally by HM King George V at Buckingham Palace on 21 July 1917. Harry passed away on 7 April 1966 and is buried in Sprowston Cemetery, near Norwich.

DAN VC

Norfolk's first recipient of the Victoria Cross during the First World War was CSM Harry Daniels, 2nd Battalion, the Rifle Brigade. Born on Market Street, Wymondham, on 13 December 1884, the thirteenth child of a local baker, tragically both his parents died while he was still a young boy and he was put in the Norwich Boys' Home on St Faith's Lane. He enlisted into the Rifle Brigade as a boy soldier and by 12 March 1915, Harry was a Company Sergeant Major in the 2nd Battalion, the Rifle Brigade at the Battle of Neuve Chappelle, France. 'A' and 'B' Companies had been virtually annihilated. Just before 5.00 p.m., 'C' and 'D' received the order to 'Attack in fifteen minutes'. Harry could see his company faced a mass of wire entanglements, the men would get caught on this and with intense machine-gun fire from the enemy it was nothing sort of suicide. Calling to his pal Corporal Cecil 'Tom' Noble, they both went over the top facing a hail of bullets to cut the wire. They were both wounded almost immediately but they kept cutting until their job was done but 'Tom' took a fatal bullet to the chest. Harry, although badly wounded, managed to crawl back. Both were awarded the Victoria Cross. After a distinguished military career, and an appearance on the British team at the 1920 Olympics, Daniels retired as a Lieutenant-Colonel in 1942 and became the manager of the Leeds Opera House. Harry died on 13 December 1953, his last request being that his ashes should be scattered on Aldershot cricket pitch.

MORE NORFOLK-BORN RECIPIENTS OF THE VC IN THE FIRST WORLD WAR

Corporal Sidney Day VC
11th Battalion, the Suffolk Regiment at Priel Wood, Malakoff Farm, east of Hargicourt, France, 26 August 1917

Corporal Day of Norwich was in command of a bombing section clearing a maze of enemy trenches. This he did, killing two machine-gunners and taking four prisoners. On reaching a point where the trench had been levelled he went alone and bombed his way through to the left in order to gain touch with the neighbouring troops. Immediately on his return to his section a stick-bomb fell into the trench occupied by two officers (one badly wounded) and three other ranks. Day seized the bomb and threw it over the trench, where it immediately exploded. This prompt action saved the lives of those in the trench. He afterwards completed the clearing of the trench and established himself in an advanced position, remaining for sixty-six hours at his post, which came under intense hostile shell, grenade, and rifle fire.

Lance Corporal Arthur Henry Cross VC, MM
40th Battalion, Machine Gun Corps at Ervillers, France, 26 March 1918

Arthur Cross, originally from Shipdham, volunteered to make a reconnaissance of the position of two machine guns which had been captured by the enemy. With the agreement of his sergeant he crept back alone with only a service revolver to what had been his section's trench. He surprised seven enemy soldiers who responded by throwing down their rifles. He then marched them carrying the machine guns complete with the tripods and ammunition to the British lines. He then handed over the prisoners and collected teams for his guns which he brought into action immediately, annihilating a very heavy attack by the enemy.

Lieutenant Gordon Flowerdew VC
Lord Strathcona's Horse, Canadian Army during 'The Last Great Cavalry Charge' at Moreuil Wood, France, 30 March 1918

Lieutenant Flowerdew of Billingford Hall near Scole, saw two lines of the enemy, each about sixty strong, with machine guns in the centre and flanks, one line being about 200 yards behind the other. Realising the critical nature of the operation and how much depended upon it, Flowerdew led three troops to charge the enemy. They passed over both lines, killing many of the enemy with the sword and, wheeling about, galloped at them again. Although the squadron had then lost about 70 per cent of its numbers, the enemy broke and retired. Lieutenant Flowerdew was dangerously wounded through both thighs during the operation but continued to cheer on his men. He died of his wounds the following day.

Lance Corporal Ernest Seaman VC, MM
2nd Battalion, the Royal Inniskilling Fusiliers, Terhand, Belgium

When the right flank of his company was being held up by enemy machine guns, Seaman went forward under heavy fire with his Lewis gun and engaged the position single-handed, capturing two machine guns, killing one officer and two men and capturing twelve prisoners. Later in the day he again rushed another enemy machine gun post, capturing the gun under very heavy fire. Ernie was killed immediately afterwards, but it was due to his gallant conduct that his company was able to push forward to its objective. Seaman had been born near Norwich and grew up at Scole.

HOLYBOY HERO

One of the most highly decorated men of the Norfolk Regiment in the First World War was Norwich soldier Sergeant Bertie James Guymer of 9th (Service) Battalion. Awarded the Military Medal in July 1917 he was awarded the bar for another brave action in June 1918. His highest award came from an action on 9 October 1918, near Bohain on the border of France and Belgium. Guymer was in charge of a platoon and led his men forward through a thick fog with great courage and ability and in spite of heavy machine-gun enfilade fire, he pushed on to his objective, surprising sixteen of the enemy in a dugout, whom he captured. In a further action on 11 October, near Vaux-Andigny, he led his platoon forward again under heavy machine-gun fire; his Company Commander recorded Guymer's 'conduct throughout was excellent' and he received the Distinguished Conduct Medal.

RETURN OF A HERO

In the churchyard of St Mary's, Suffield, lies Private William Thirst. A local lad, he went away to war and was awarded the Military Medal 'For Bravery in the Field' while serving with the 7th Battalion, the Royal Sussex Regiment. Wounded in action, he was evacuated back to Blighty and Cardiff Hospital where, sadly, he succumbed to his injuries on 4 October 1918, little more than a month before the end of the First World War. Returned to Suffield for burial in his family plot, he is named on the family headstone. He also has a Commonwealth War Graves Commission headstone next to the grave. His younger brother John was also killed during the war.

THE PITY OF WAR

There were sixty-two auxiliary hospitals set up in Norfolk during the First World War. Between them they provided 1,377 beds, through which passed 27,446 convalescent soldiers who were cared for by a total of 35,736 VAD nurses, orderlies, drivers and volunteers drawn from both the British Red Cross Society and Order of St John in the county.

The main YMCA centre that provided comforts and entertainments for troops in St Andrew's Hall, Norwich, was used, on average, by some 20,000 soldiers every week.

Only one man fell from the village of Ingworth during the First World War. He was Private Eustace Campbell Kaufmann who was serving with the 46th Battalion, the Canadian Infantry (Saskatchewan Regiment). Born at Ingworth, the son of the rector he had emigrated before the war. A bronze tablet was erected by the parishioners to his memory in the church.

In 1920 the Norfolk Roll of Honour was published with returns from 626 of the 700 Norfolk parishes; it showed some 11,771 Norfolk men and women lost their lives in the war, over 2,200 of them were from Norwich. In its statistical summary it was estimated that out of the total number of Norfolk people who served, the proportion of them missing or killed was about 1 in 9.

Out of the 20,000 or so English parishes which saw their young men and women serve in the First World War, only thirty-one saw them all return: Ovington was one of them. Twelve boys marched away to war and all twelve returned. It is believed Ovington is the only village or town in Norfolk to have this claim.

TWO SECOND WORLD WAR FIRSTS

The 2nd Battalion, the Royal Norfolk Regiment was the first complete infantry unit of the British Expeditionary Force to land in France. It was also members of the 2nd Battalion, the Royal Norfolk Regiment who were awarded the first army decorations during the Second World War when Captain Peter Barclay and Corporal M.H. 'Mick' Davis were respectively granted the Military Cross and Military Medal for their gallantry during a scouting mission and subsequent contact with the enemy on the night of 3/4 January 1940.

ON THE HOME FRONT

The first test blackout was conducted for the entire county between the hours of midnight on the night of 13 July and 4.00 a.m. on 14 July 1939.

The provisions provided for the children evacuated to Norfolk on 1 September 1939 included: 976 cases of tinned milk, 21,000lb of biscuits, 73,000 cases of chocolate and 21,000 carrier bags.

Within two weeks of the initial appeal for volunteers by Antony Eden on 14 May 1940, some 30,000 Norfolk men had volunteered for the Local Defence Volunteers.

The twenty Church Army canteen vans in Norwich served 10,000 cups of tea during the air raids of April 1942.

By May 1944 there were over 1,650 members of the Women's Land Army working in Norfolk.

During the flying bomb blitz of September 1944, an estimated 20,000 evacuees were sent to Norfolk.

MAGNA MAGIC

A unique organisation was established in Norwich between July 1940 and August 1941. The Mutual Aid Good Neighbours Association (M.A.G.N.A.) was raised with the intention of cooperating with the ARP and other organisations to provide aid for the victims of air raids, particularly those who were suffering from shock and to alleviate the distress of those rendered homeless as a result of being bombed out. Staffed along the lines of the ARP an appeal was launched for over 2,000 volunteers to find a 'Street Mother' for every street. The Organiser for the City was the indefatigable Mrs Ruth Hardy who saw M.A.G.N.A. grow to over 30,000 Norwich women who offered their home as shelter and temporary accommodation to their neighbours.

JAM AND JERUSALEM

In 1940, despite only having forty-eight members, the Morningthorpe, Fritton and District branch of the Women's Institute, knitted approximately 1,000 comforts and 16 blankets supplied to men serving in the forces from the village, Red Cross and St John, Royal Navy and Minesweepers. They raised £22 for wool, received thirty evacuees into their homes and collected clothing for their benefit. They maintained a weekly supply of vegetables to the forces and the Savings Groups started by their branch saved £150 15s. In addition to this, the branch made up articles for hospitals, helped with salvage and their Preserving Centre made 1,650lb of jam and jelly.

THE CRUEL SEA

At the outbreak of war the Great Yarmouth base became HMS *Watchful* and provided convoys with protection from Motor Torpedo Boats (MTBs), salvage tugs and Air Sea Rescue boats. In 1940 HMS *Miranda* was established as a dedicated base for the minesweeping trawlers at the Fishwharf.

From 1 January 1941 to 21 July 1945, HMS *Midge* became Yarmouth's coastal forces base under Commander E.R. Lewis DSO, DSC with responsibility for MTBs, Motor Gun Boats (MGBs) and Mine Layers.

When enemy aircraft dropped six high explosive bombs across the southern part of Great Yarmouth at 6.28 a.m. on Thursday 18 March 1943, the HMS *Midge* WRNS billet at the corner of Queen's Road and Nelson Road South received a direct hit. Rescue parties were rapidly on the scene and despite their work being hampered by a fire breaking out in the debris, they managed to pull thirteen Wrens alive from the wreckage. The bodies of eight less fortunate Wrens were also recovered.

MINE!

During the invasion scares of 1940, miles of beaches around the East Coast and both The Wash and the Norfolk Broads were mined.

The mines on Trimingham beach took decades to clear after the end of the war. Successive troops of Royal Engineers charged with this dangerous job remained on site until the early 1970s when the beach and cliffs were finally returned to the local community.

A unique memorial to the Royal Engineer Bomb Disposal personnel who were killed while clearing land mines on the Norfolk coast from 1944 to 1953 was dedicated by Sir Timothy Colman KG, HM Lord Lieutenant of Norfolk at Mundesley on 2 May 2004.

DANGER UXB

By a remarkable coincidence, on the same day that the George Medal was introduced, on 24 September 1940, men of 8 Section, 4 Bomb Disposal Company, the Royal Engineers went to work on a 250kg bomb which had smashed through the path and embedded itself 30ft down into the soft subsoil outside no. 4 Theatre Street, Norwich. It took a total of four days to uncover and defuse the bomb; it had been no easy task and one that could so easily have resulted in death and destruction. In December 1940, in an unparalleled awards ceremony for a single act, three members of the section were awarded the George Medal for their roles in the successful disposal of this device.

WORST-HIT TOWN ON THE EAST COAST

The year 1941 saw Great Yarmouth suffer its worst year of bombing. A total 767 alerts were sounded and 1,328 'crash' warnings given. A total of 167 raids were conducted on the town during the course of which 803 high explosive bombs and six mines exploded in the borough, destroying many of the old 'Rows'. An estimated 7,020 incendiary bombs rained down and 55 UXBs had to be dealt with by bomb disposal squads. 109 people lost their lives, 329 were injured and the historic townscape of Great Yarmouth was changed forever.

BRAVE BROTHERS

Derek and Hugh Seagrim, sons of the Revd Charles Seagrim, rector of Whissonsett, have the unique distinction of being the only brothers ever to receive our country's highest awards for bravery – the VC and the GC. Lieutenant-Colonel Derek Seagrim was in command of 7th Battalion, the Green Howards when his courage and leadership in action led to the capture of an important objective on the Mareth Line in Tunisia on 20/21 March 1943. Tragically, the award of his Victoria Cross was made posthumously after Derek died on 6 April 1943 from wounds he had the Battle of Wadi Akarit.

Major Hugh Seagrim led the Karen rebels when the Japanese invaded Burma, but their acts of sabotage and guerilla attacks resulted in bloody reprisals against the Karen people and to prevent further bloodshed, Hugh surrendered himself in March 1944. After enduring appalling treatment in Japanese captivity, Hugh and eight of his Karen compatriots were executed at Rangoon on 22 September 1944. He was posthumously awarded the George Cross in 1946 for his gallantry under captivity.

VCs OF THE ROYAL NORFOLK REGIMENT

The Royal Norfolk Regiment was awarded five Victoria Crosses during the Second World War – a record unsurpassed by any other county regiment in that conflict, the recipients were:

CSM George Gristock VC: 2nd Battalion, River Escaut, near Tournai, Belgium, 21 May 1940

Acting Corporal Sidney 'Basher' Bates VC: 1st Battalion, Pavée, Sourdeval, France, 6 August 1944

Captain David Jamieson VC: 7th Battalion, Orne Bridgehead, Grimbosq, Normandy, France, 7/8 August 1944

Captain John Niel 'Jack' Randle VC: 2nd Battalion, GPT Ridge, Kohima, Assam (north-east India), 6 May 1944

Lieutenant George Arthur Knowland attached No. 1 Commando, Kangaw, Burma, 31 January 1945

Only David Jamieson lived to receive his award, all other Norfolk VCs were awarded posthumously.

IN THE AIR

The first Observer Corps posts in Norfolk were established at Mundesley and Wymondham in 1934.

The first German aircraft to crash on Norfolk during the Second World War was a Heinkel He 115 float plane (2081) from 3/Küstenfliegergruppe (Maritime Group) 506 that crashed onto the West Beach, Sheringham, at 3.15 a.m. on 6 December 1939. All crew were killed. Had this aircraft crashed above the high water mark it would have been the first enemy aircraft to crash on British soil in the Second World War.

Blue Cock 'Royal Blue', bred by and trained at HM King George VI's Pigeon Loft, Sandringham, and operating out of RAF Bircham Newton, was the first pigeon to bring a message from a force-landed aircrew on the continent during the Second World War. Released by the crew in Holland on 10 October 1940 at 07.20 hours, the young bird arrived with its message at Sandringham at 11.30 hours the same day. This efficient pigeon was recognised for this action by the award of the Dickin Medal – 'the animals' VC' – in March 1945.

Second World War hero Douglas Bader flew from RAF Coltishall as a squadron leader with 242 Squadron during the Battle of Britain in 1940.

In the Commonwealth War Graves Cemetery at Coltishall is one of the most unusual casualties to be marked by the CWGC anywhere in the world. The inscription names 'O.W. Kanturek, Twentieth Century Fox'. Otto Walter Kanturek was renowned Hollywood cinematographer who was tragically killed on 26 June 1941. While capturing the final aerial shots for *A Yank in the RAF*, the Hurricane fighter that was to dive past the camera plane collided with it. The pilot of the Hurricane managed to bail out and survived but all of those in the camera plane, including Otto Kanturek, did not survive the crash.

The first USAAF heavy bomber base in the county was opened at Shipdam in October 1942.

Hollywood film star James Stewart served as a captain in 445th Bombardment Group USAAF flying B-24 Liberators bombers at Tibenham, and after promotion to major in March 1944 was transferred to 453rd Bombardment Group at Old Buckenham as their Group Executive Officer.

In June 1944 Major Glenn Miller and the 8th AAF Band began their month-long tour across the airfields and venues of East Anglia, including performances at the bases at Attlebridge, Hardwick, Thorpe Abbotts, Wendling and at the Samson and Hercules in Norwich.

Of the American servicemen assigned to this region, 6,700 men of the 2nd Air Division of the United States 8th Air Force were killed in action flying from local airfields.

In 1944, a USAAF bomber crew training in thick fog hit the flagpole on St Philip's Church on Heigham Road, Norwich. The pilot, Second Lieutenant Ralph Dooley, flying low over rooftops and desperately struggling to avoid landing on the houses below, eventually crashed on waste ground near Barker Street. All the crew perished, but their heroism in saving civilian lives was recognised by local residents who erected a memorial plaque near the spot in their memory.

The first V1 to fall on the county landed at Ovington on 10 July 1944. The first V2 crashed into the county on a field near Ranworth at 4.25 p.m. on 26 September 1944.

340 people died during the air raids on Norwich during the Second World War. Over 30,000 houses were damaged, 2,000 of them beyond repair.

THE BOYS *(AND GIRL)* OF THE OLD BRIGADE

Charles Boyles, Vice Admiral of the Blue, a man who commenced his career with Nelson aboard the *Raisonnable* and the man after whom Boyles Point in British Columbia was named, was born at Wells in 1756.

Thomas Troughton, the last member of the loyal corps of artillery raised for the defence of Norwich during the 1745 rebellion, died at St George's Colegate in February 1806 aged eighty-eight.

When Lieutenant-General James Hethersett died on 15 April 1812 he was the last surviving officer who fought by the side of General Wolfe at the Battle of Quebec in 1759. Ironically, Samuel Mog, one of the last other surviving ranks of the battle, died a few days later at Corpusty aged 104. The last Norfolk veteran of the Battle of Quebec was John Hoy of Hackford who died in January 1817, and had been present at the battle as part of the 48th Regiment of Foot.

When John Folker died aged eighty-six in May 1838 he was the last of a number of King's Lynn seamen who served at the Battle of the Saintes, 12 April 1782. Folker had been Admiral Rodney's flagship helmsman throughout the battle where glorious victory was achieved over the French fleet. He was buried with full honours in St Mary's churchyard.

The first keeper of the Nelson Monument at Great Yarmouth was James Sharman, a local man who had been press-ganged into the navy at the age of fourteen. He was serving as an ordinary seaman aboard HMS *Victory* at the Battle of Trafalgar and had helped carry Nelson below when he was fatally wounded. In 1827, Sharman performed an act of great bravery in rescuing the crew of the brig *Hammond* that was wrecked on the beach near his cottage. Charles Dickens read the newspaper report and was moved to visit Sharman in Yarmouth and based his character, Ham Peggotty in *David Copperfield*, on him. James Sharman remained as 'Keeper of the Pillar' from 1819 until his death in 1867.

In Knapton churchyard is the gravestone of Commander Jeffreson Miles RN. It is inscribed with the legend 'the vindicator of Nelson'. This is quite true – after Nelson's death the national hero's name was besmirched with claims that he had mistreated Republican prisoners while at Naples in 1799. Commander Miles wrote a pamphlet clearly pointing out that Nelson had acted with authority and that our hero's name was being tarnished with lies and misunderstandings.

Thomas Harrison was born in Norwich in 1796, he joined the 69th Regiment aged seventeen and was taken prisoner at the bombardment of Antwerp. He was present at Waterloo, served in India and took part in the first expedition into Burma. On his return to England he was awarded an honourable discharge with a pension of 15*d* per day. He lived out his later years back in Norwich and died on 29 March 1886.

James 'Old Balaclava' Olley was just sixteen years old and serving with the 4th Light Dragoons when he took part in the Charge of the Light Brigade on 25 October 1854. He lived to be the last Norfolk survivor of the infamous charge when he died at Elsing in 1920.

One of the last Norfolk survivors of the Battle of Trafalgar was Commander Francis Harris RN who was serving as a first class volunteer gunner aboard the *Temeraire*. He died at Southtown, Great Yarmouth, on 9 July 1883.

John 'Jackie' Fisher (1841–1920), distinguished Admiral and First Sea Lord, is buried in the churchyard of Kilverstone, his country seat.

William Francis Burman was a Stepney-born twenty-year-old sergeant in 16th Battalion, the Rifle Brigade when he won his Victoria Cross during the Battle of Passchendaele on 20 September 1917. When the advance of his company was held up by a machine gun at point-blank range, Sergeant Burman had shouted to the men next to him to wait a few minutes and going forward to what seemed certain death, killed the enemy gunner and carried the gun to the company's objective where he used it with great effect. Fifteen minutes later it was seen that about forty of the enemy were enfilading the battalion on the right. Sergeant Burman and two others ran and got behind them, killing six and capturing two officers and twenty-nine other ranks. Sergeant William Francis Burman VC died at Cromer on 23 October 1974.

The late Henry Allingham who died in 2009 aged 113 was, at the time, the world's (verifiable) oldest man, and the last man alive to have served in the Royal Naval Air Service during the First World War. He served at both Bacton and Great Yarmouth RNAS stations in the early years of the war as an air mechanic.

Florence Beatrice Green (née Patterson), born 19 February 1901, is the last known female veteran of the First World War. She is also the third oldest military veteran in the world and one of the twenty oldest people in Britain. Born in London, Florence joined the Women's Royal Air Force in September 1918 at the age of seventeen and served as a waitress working in the officers' mess at RAF Marham and at Narborough Airfield. She moved to King's Lynn in 1920, after her marriage to Walter Green, a railway worker who died in 1970 after fifty years of marriage. At the time of writing she still lives in King's Lynn with her daughter May, who was born in 1921.

3

CRIME & PUNISHMENT

CONSTABULARY DUTIES

A private watch (a type of early police) formed and funded by the inhabitants of St Stephen's, Norwich, commenced its duties in November 1824.

The new police were on duty for the first time in Norwich on 1 March 1836. Constables were paid 15s a week with a stoppage of 1s for clothing – even though they had to provide their own trousers.

Norfolk Rural Police Force was founded on 22 November 1839. Divided into twelve areas across the county, it began with just twelve superintendents and 120 constables.

The first crime statistics for the new Norwich Police ran from 25 December 1837 to 25 December 1838. These show the force, over a period of twelve months, dealt with a total of 69 felonies, 56 assaults, 113 disorderly persons and 5 cases of uttering false coins.

On 23 June 1846 PC William Callow of Norwich City Police was the first Norfolk police officer to die from injuries sustained in the course of his duties. He received head injuries from an angry mob throwing large stones, bottles and sticks while Callow and a number of his colleagues were escorting refractory paupers from the workhouse on St Andrew's Hill to the City Gaol.

On 18 August 1909 PC37 Charles Alger of Great Yarmouth Borough Police was the first Norfolk police constable to be fatally shot in the line of duty. He had been summoned to St Andrew's Road, Gorleston, where Thomas Allen, a local ne'er do well, was behaving in a threatening manner with a shotgun. PC Alger was invited into the garden to discuss the matter by the unarmed Allen, who at once picked up the shotgun he had hidden in his potato patch and discharged the weapon at Alger at point-blank range.

On 17 November 1888 a letter was received by Great Yarmouth police purporting to come from Jack the Ripper. Its threat to 'rip up two Norwich women' near one of the piers was leaked and panic set in across the town. A large crowd was drawn to the scene but Jack failed to appear.

RIOTOUS ASSEMBLIES

In his *Historia Anglicana*, Bartholomew Cotton recounts:

> 1272, on the day following the Feast of St Laurence [11 August], the
> citizens of Norwich laid siege around the precincts of the monastery.
> When their insults failed to gain them admittance, they set fire to
> the main gate into the monastery . . . they burned the dormitory,
> the refectory, the guest hall, the infirmary with its chapel and indeed
> almost all the buildings within the precincts of the monastery.
> This killed many members of the monastery's household, some sub
> deacons and clerics and some lay people in the cloister and in the
> monastery. Others they dragged off and put to death in the city.

The high prices and scarcity of grain caused a number of riots to break out at a number of places across the county over the years. On 23 August 1740 thousands took to the streets in Norwich, King's Lynn, Yarmouth and other locations to protest with the properties and premises associated with millers and bakers being the main targets. In a number of cases the rioters turned nasty; properties were damaged, people were threatened and violence broke out. Soldiers were called upon to restore order. At Norwich the troops fired on the crowd killing seven, including the young man assumed to be the ringleader, and wounding a number more.

A dreadful riot occurred in Norwich on 27 September 1766 on account of the great scarcity and price of provisions, especially corn. The houses of bakers were damaged, a large malthouse outside Conesford Gate was burned and a Tombland baker's house was totally destroyed. The riot was quelled by 'magistrates and citizens'. Thirty 'ringleaders' were tried, eight were sentenced to death but only two (John Hall and David Long) went to the gallows.

The first instance of machine-breaking in Norfolk occurred on 19 May 1816 when over 100 labourers assembled and riotously destroyed a threshing machine belonging to William Burlingham at Hockham.

When Downham Market agricultural labourers demanded wages of 2s per day be paid every Monday and Thursday, their farmer employers refused and the situation rapidly escalated into a riot in the town on 20 May 1816. Armed with clubs and other weapons, the rioters smashed windows and raided shops and stores. The situation was only quelled after Upwell Cavalry were called out and the Riot Act read. On 24 May another disturbance took place when two women and several men accused of being rioters were removed from the town to Norwich Castle. Brought before the Assizes, nine men and six women were found guilty and sentenced to death. Most of them were respited but Daniel Harwood and Thomas Thody went to the gallows.

On 12 June 1827 weavers rioted in Norwich. Only after the Riot Act was read and a mounted charge was made did the crowd disperse and order return. Militia were under arms on Castle Hill and street patrols were carried out by the Norwich Light Horse Volunteers.

Infamous Norfolk rebel Richard Nockolds, the man who had led weavers' riots in Norwich and labourers' riots in the county in 1830 was finally captured, tried, found guilty and executed on 9 April 1831 for setting fire to hay stacks at Swanton Abbot.

ROUGH JUSTICE

The first to be burned for heresy in Lollard's Pit in Norwich were William Wyatt, William Waddon and Hugh Pye in 1427. The first Protestant martyr to be burned there was Thomas Bilney on 19 August 1531. He was followed by many more during the reign of 'Bloody' Queen Mary. The last heretic to be burned at Norwich was John Lewes who met his end on 18 September 1583 in the castle ditches having been found guilty of blasphemy.

A maidservant was boiled to death at the Tuesday Market Place in King's Lynn in 1531, for the crime of poisoning her mistress.

In 1566 Richard Ingham refused to plead guilty or not guilty to a felony. His trial could not proceed without a plea so he was pressed to give an answer – literally. Ingham was tied spread-eagled to the floor and weights were gradually piled upon his chest without relief. Given the option of plead or die he persisted in his refusal and his life ended 'under the press'.

Matthew Hamond, a Hethersett wheelwright, was an obstinate heretic and blasphemer. Found guilty of 'reviling the Queen's Majesty and denying the doctrine of the Trinity' he was put in the pillory on 13 May 1578 in Norwich Market Place and both his ears were nailed. He was burned in the Castle Ditch the following week.

In 1615 Catholic priest Thomas Tunstall was hanged, drawn and quartered upon the gallows by Magdalen Gate. His head was then set upon a pole on St Benedict's Gate and his quarters displayed upon four other gates of the city.

In July 1809 George Hubbard was publicly whipped in Norwich Market Place and he suffered six months' solitary confinement for stealing a pair of velveteen breeches.

On 28 September 1708 Michael Hammond, aged seven, and his sister Ann, aged eleven, were convicted of stealing of a loaf of bread in King's Lynn and were sentenced to death.

In October 1823 William Burton Peeling, a prisoner at Swaffham Gaol, was attempting to hold an illicit conversation with another prisoner in the adjoining division as they walked the treadmill. Peeling became so absorbed while talking that he bent his head too far forward and he was drawn into the wheel with the result that he was crushed to death.

GO TO JAIL

On 2 September 1756, after a six-hour naval engagement off Lowestoft between HMS *Hazard* and a French privateer, *La Subtille*, the Frenchman struck off Winterton. The crew were taken prisoner, landed and lodged in the Tolhouse Gaol. By undermining the prison wall, fourteen broke out but only four were retaken. There is no record of what happened to the rest; perhaps their descendants are still among us?

Elizabeth Fry (née Gurney), prison and social reformer, Quaker and Christian philanthropist was born in Gurney Court, off Magdalen Street in Norwich, on 21 May 1780.

Mary Hudson (aged thirty-five) escaped from Norwich Gaol under extraordinary circumstances on 9 November 1808. Her cell wall was 2ft thick and over a number of nights Mary had worked the bricks out, hiding them under her bed, secreting loose rubbish in her pillow and using another bed case to hide the hole. Once she had made a sufficient hole in the wall, Hudson crept out into the street taking her six-month-old infant with her, and despite a reward of 10 guineas being offered, there is no record of her recapture.

Highwaymen John and William Brooks tried to escape from the cell in Bigod's Tower in Norwich Castle in February 1835. Their improvised rope made from a blanket and rug gave way causing William to plummet 70ft to the ground. Despite his thighs, pelvis, left arm and ribs on his left side being broken and a large swelling forming at the back of his head, he recovered and was sentenced to transportation for life.

Henry Pettett was a prisoner under sentence of transportation for horse stealing, when he made his escape bid from Norwich Castle Prison on 22 March 1838. He fashioned a rope from his blanket, let himself out and proceeded to the top of the castle but failed to get away when he fell down and pitched his head into a bucket causing himself a serious injury.

The new prison built to replace the old Norwich Castle Prison (for Norfolk felons) and the Old Norwich City Gaol, was opened on Prison Road (now Knox Road), Norwich, on 16 July 1887.

On 11 February 1888 notorious Norfolk poacher Robert Large, with another prisoner named Annison, were the first prisoners to escape from the new HMP Norwich. Both were later recaptured.

Notorious 'Great Train Robber' Ronnie Biggs was moved from Belmarsh Prison to Norwich Prison in July 2007 until his release on compassionate grounds in 2009.

Reggie Kray was serving the last period of his sentence at Wayland Prison in Norfolk when he was released on compassionate grounds as he was suffering from cancer. He died a few weeks after his release on 1 October 2000 at the Town House Hotel in Thorpe St Andrew.

HANGING AROUND

The last hanging conducted at Wymondham was that of Robert Basset and William Boughton on 1 April 1713. Both had been convicted for being party to the murder of James Pointer on 8 October 1712.

The last gibbet in Yarmouth contained the body of William Payne the pirate. After swinging for twenty-three years on the North Denes it was finally taken down by order of the Corporation on 2 May 1804.

The last person hanged at Great Yarmouth was seventy-year-old John Hannah who was executed on 6 September 1813 for murdering his wife.

Frances Billing and Catherine Frary – 'The Burnham Poisoners' – were executed in front of Norwich Castle on 10 August 1835. This would prove be the last public double execution of women in the county. They were also the last women to hang in Norfolk.

The last public execution in Norfolk was carried out on 26 August 1867 by executioner William Calcraft in front of Norwich Castle when he hanged Hubbard Lingley for the murder of his uncle Benjamin Black at Barton Bendish.

John Thurston was convicted of the murder of an old man, Henry Springall, at Hingham on 5 December 1885 and was executed at Norwich Castle. Thurston was a nephew of Henry Webster who had been hanged at the same prison on 1 May 1876 for the murder of his wife at Cranworth.

During the execution of wife-killer Robert Goodale by hanging conducted at Norwich Castle Gaol on 30 November 1885, Goodale's head was torn off by the rope. The executioner, James Berry, was acquitted of fault but the incident was known to executioners ever after as 'The Goodale Mess'. Charles Mackie, who was present at the execution as a representative of the press always said, with some pride, he was present at 'the last judicial decapitation in Britain'.

The last person to hang at Norwich Castle was George Harmer on 13 December 1886. Harmer had killed Henry Last at Norwich during a robbery.

The first man to hang at the new HMP Norwich off Plumstead Road was George Watt on 12 July 1898. He was given an appointment with the executioner for shooting his wife Sophia at Denmark Terrace, Sprowston Road, Norwich.

4

NORFOLK PEOPLE: FAMOUS & NOT SO

PRIDE OF NORFOLK

Boudicca, Queen of the Iceni, ruled over a kingdom that extended over much of modern Norfolk and into our neighbouring counties. Truly formidable in battle, she led the rebellion against the Roman occupiers in AD 60 or 61, sacking the main Roman settlements of Camulodunum (Colchester), Londinium (London) and Verulamium (St Albans).

Sir Thomas Browne (1605–82) physician and philosopher, the author of *Religio Medici* (the Religion of a Physician) – the first defence and contemplation of the medical profession in modern literature – and a number of other books on religion, science and the esoteric, spent most of his life in Norwich.

Sir Robert Walpole, 1st Earl of Orford, the statesman generally regarded as having been the first Prime Minister of Great Britain, was born at Houghton Hall in 1676.

Although it is debated if Anne Boleyn (1507–36) was actually born in Norfolk, she certainly spent some of her young life at Blickling Hall, near Aylsham. She became the second wife of King Henry VIII, presented him with a fine daughter (who became Elizabeth I) but produced no male heir. Convicted of trumped-up charges of adultery and treason, Anne was beheaded (by sword at her own request) on 19 May 1536.

Captain George Vancouver RN, who led the expedition to explore North America's north-western Pacific Coast regions including the coasts of contemporary Alaska, British Columbia, Washington and Oregon, was born at King's Lynn in 1757. Captain Vancouver originally claimed Alaska for the Crown under the name of 'New Norfolk' but this was not to be. He is however immortalised in the place name of Vancouver in British Columbia and introduced such local place names as Lynn, Point Snettisham and Holkham Bay to those foreign shores. Vancouver Island, Canada; the cities of Vancouver, British Columbia, Canada, and Vancouver, Washington in the United States and Mount Vancouver on the Yukon/Alaskan border are all so named in his honour.

Thomas Fowell Buxton (1786–1845), slavery abolitionist, took over as leader of the Abolition Movement in the British House of Commons after William Wilberforce retired in 1825. His efforts paid off in 1833 when slavery was officially abolished, freeing the 700,000 slaves then held in the West Indies and across the British Empire. Buxton spent his last years of life at Northrepps Hall.

Sir Astley Paston Cooper, the eminent surgeon and anatomist who made significant contributions to vascular and hernia surgery, the anatomy and pathology of the mammary glands and testicles, received a baronetcy for removing a small tumour from the scalp of George IV. Cooper was born at Brooke Hall in 1768.

Yarmouth-born Anna Sewell (1820–78) produced her only book, the children's classic *Black Beauty*, a year before she died. Anna is buried at the Quaker Chapel, Lamas.

Howard Carter, the man who discovered the tomb of Tutankhamun in 1922, spent most of his youth at Swaffham.

Francis Blomefield (1705–52) Rector of Fersfield was the author of the first major work on the history of Norfolk which he printed on his own press. He got as far as page 678 of the third volume when he was struck down with the smallpox that was to prove fatal for him. Fortunately his work was continued and completed by Charles Parkyn, the Rector of Oxborough.

ROYAL CONNECTIONS

John Caius was born at Norwich on 5 October 1510. He went on to become President of the College of Physicians nine times and physician to Edward VI, Queen Mary and Queen Elizabeth.

Tilney St Lawrence-born John Aylmer (1521–94) was tutor to Lady Jane Grey – queen for just nine days. Aylmer feared for his own life too and fled to the continent to avoid the persecution of Mary Tudor. He returned when Elizabeth I ascended the throne and eventually became Bishop of London.

Sir Charles Scarburgh, court physician to Charles II, James II and William III was the son of Edmund Scarburgh, a native of North Walsham.

Dr Robert Brady (1627–1700), academic, historical writer and physician to Charles II and James II, was born at Denver.

Sir James Paget (1814–99), Surgeon Extraordinary to the Queen and Surgeon in Ordinary to the Prince of Wales, was born at Great Yarmouth.

King Louis XVIII, travelling as Count de Lille, arrived off Yarmouth in a Swedish frigate and landed on 2 November 1807. He was accompanied by other representatives of the French nobility fleeing the terror, including the Duc d'Angoulême and the Duc de Berry.

Gustav IV Adolf, the ex-King of Sweden, travelling under the title of Count Gottorp, landed under a royal salute at Great Yarmouth on 12 November 1810. Gustav Adolf's inept and erratic leadership in diplomacy and war had precipitated his abdication.

Dr Charles Browne, who held the position of physician to the King of Prussia for many years and was presented with the Order of the Red Eagle as a mark of esteem, ended his days in Norfolk, at Margaretta Farm, Clenchwarton, where he died in May 1827 aged eighty-three.

William Norman, who died at Windsor Place, New Lakenham, in May 1842, had served many years as hairdresser to His Late Majesty King George III.

In 1908 a bungalow was built on the northern side of Snettisham beach for Queen Alexandra, wife of King Edward VII. It was built in a style to resemble houses in the queen's homeland of Denmark. Accompanied by her entourage of servants and occasionally visited by friends, the queen loved her little cottage by the sea but after her death in 1925 it sadly it fell into disrepair and was eventually demolished.

King Edward VII paid what was to be his last official visit to Norwich on 25 October 1909 where he was greeted by thousands of schoolchildren singing on Mousehold. He presented colours and reviewed the 3,000-strong Territorial Force and a parade of veterans from the Royal Norfolk Veterans Association.

The front rank of the Queen's Golden Jubilee parade in London on 4 June 2002 contained three members of one family from Norfolk: St John Ambulance County Sergeant Major Neil Storey, his son Lawrence (then aged nine), and Neil's partner Molly Housego.

HAVE YOU HEARD OF . . . ?

Norfolk knight Sir John Fastolf (1378–1459) of Caister Hall, who served with distinction during the Hundred Years War, was one of the inspirations for William Shakespeare's character Sir John Falstaff.

Robert Paul, formerly of Starston, was the renowned inventor of several devices for enquiry into the nature, history and habitudes of turnip fly and wireworm. He died at Harleston in April 1827.

Robert Cutting had been the postman between Swainsthorpe and Norwich for fifty years when he died in 1834. His achievement was all the more remarkable because he was quite blind but 'Blind Bob' could find any place he was sent in the city.

Dr Allan Glaiser Minns, elected Mayor of the Borough of Thetford in 1904, was Britain's first black mayor. Alan was born on 19 October 1858 in the Bahamas, he later studied at Guy's Hospital in London and became the Medical Officer at Thetford Workhouse and for Thetford Cottage Hospital.

Sarah Jessup served Winfarthing as a walking postwoman between the village and Diss, a distance of 4 miles, for thirty years. When she died it was calculated she had walked a total of 13,400 miles and was still performing her duties until she died aged 101 in February 1833.

William Cubitt was born at Dilham, where his father was a miller, in 1785. The family later moved to Southrepps, then to Bacton

Wood Mill, near North Walsham. A self-taught but enormously skilled engineer, Cubitt invented self-regulating windmill sails, engineered canals such as the Norwich & Lowestoft Navigation and the Shropshire Union Canal, and acted as consultant engineer to the South Eastern Railway. He was consultant engineer for the building of the Crystal Palace and for this work he received a knighthood. However, he will be best remembered for one of his earliest and most infamous inventions – the prison tread wheel.

Richard Barcham Shalders was born at Worstead in 1824. A hard-working and devoutly religious man, he emigrated to New Zealand in 1852 and within a year he became the founder of the New Zealand branch of the YMCA and founder of Auckland Baptist Tabernacle in 1855.

Sarah Ann Glover (1785–1867) was born in The Close and lived in Norwich for many years. While there she created tonic sol-fa, a pedagogical technique for teaching sight-singing (*do, reh, me,* etc).

Tom and Annie 'Kitty' Higdon were the teachers at the centre of the Burston School Strike. The situation arose when Tom became involved in trade union activities and the couple had tried to improve the conditions in the school, only to end up being sacked in April 1914. But the children would not let this happen without a fight and sixty-six of the school's seventy children came out on strike. A new school was begun with the Higdons in a marquee on the village green. The school then moved to local carpenter's premises and later to a purpose-built school financed by donations from the labour movement. Burston Strike School carried on teaching local children until shortly after Tom's death in 1939.

Captain Samuel Gurney Cresswell, the first naval officer to cross the entire Northwest Passage, was born at King's Lynn on 25 September 1827.

Humphry Repton, whose masterpieces of landscaping may still be seen at some of the great houses and finest residences in the country, died on 24 March 1818 and is buried in Aylsham churchyard. Not far from him, in the same churchyard, is Joseph Clover (1825–82) the man described as 'the Father of modern anaesthetics'. Clover developed the first apparatus to provide chloroform in controlled concentrations in 1862.

Dr Edward Rigby (1747–1821) was associated with the Norfolk and Norwich Hospital for fifty years from its foundation in 1771 and was responsible for introducing vaccination into the city.

Dr William Guy saved many lives in Norwich when he bravely took medical charge of the isolation hospital during the smallpox outbreak in 1871. Afterwards appointed to the post of public vaccinator, it was said for years after that Norwich was 'the best vaccinated town in the kingdom'.

Harold Davidson (1876–1937) the rector of Stiffkey and Morston for twenty-six years, became known as 'the Prostitutes' Padre' for his work with fallen women in London. Well loved by most of his parishioners Davidson's work was not popular with all, and some ill-founded accusations became blown out of proportion. After a Church disciplinary trial he was defrocked in 1932. Davidson spent the rest of his life campaigning against the injustice he had suffered and used amusement parks and circuses as his platform. He died at Skegness from injuries he suffered after being mauled while delivering an oration from a cage of lions.

The infamous Dr Hawley Harvey Crippen, the first criminal to be caught thanks to wireless telegraphy, hanged in Pentonville Prison, London, on 23 November 1910 for the murder of his wife, Cora. Crippen shared his appearances in court and the spotlight of the media with his mistress Ethel le Neve, who had tried to escape with him while disguised as his son. Few realised she had been born plain Ethel Neave on Bryers Lane, off Victoria Road, Diss, in January 1883. She was acquitted of all charges and died in obscurity.

THE LONG AND THE SHORT OF IT

Robert Hales, the celebrated Norfolk Giant, stood 7ft 8in tall and measured 64in around his waist in his prime. Introduced to Queen Victoria and other dignitaries and weighing in at 33 stone, he toured America but eventually gave it up to settle down to become a publican. He eventually returned to Norfolk and lived in a caravan at Cumber Corner at Beighton and lived his last years in Great Yarmouth. Sadly his health deteriorated and he was reduced to selling leaflets about

his life and times in Norwich and Yarmouth. Hales died of bronchitis on 22 November 1863 aged forty-three at his home on Wellington Road, Great Yarmouth, and was returned to his place of birth for burial in St Mary's churchyard, West Somerton. His sister Mary was also tall: she stood 7ft 2in and toured some early shows with Robert. Their parents William and Ann Hales raised nine children, whose joint heights amounted to 57ft 6in.

Joan Coan was known as 'The Norfolk Pigmy'. Born at Tivetshall in 1728, she stopped growing while she was still a child and toured with local fairs where she displayed herself entertaining her audience with song and dance routines. When she was measured in 1759 Joan stood just 38in high in her hat and boots and weighed 38lb. Working long hours in her performances, Joan's health began to deteriorate and she died in 1764. Showman John Pinchbeck displayed her corpse as a curiosity after her death but was eventually forced to bury her and exhibited a waxwork model instead.

THE AMERICAN CONNECTION

Temperance Flowerdew left Hethersett to sail to Virginia in 1609. She married George Yardley, later Sir George Yardley, the Governor of Virginia, so Temperance therefore became the first titled lady of America.

Samuel Lincoln was baptised at Hingham church, and later became apprenticed to a Norwich weaver. In the spring of 1638 he and his master sailed from Great Yarmouth and arrived in Salem, Massachusetts, at the end of June. The Lincoln family moved from Hingham, Massachusetts, to Pennsylvania, then to Virginia, eventually settling in Kentucky, where Abraham Lincoln was born.

Sir William Gooch, Governor of Virginia in the USA (1727–49), the man who negotiated the Treaty of Lancaster which insured protection from the Indian tribes to the north and west of the colony, was born in Great Yarmouth.

Thomas Willet, the first Mayor of New York City (1665–6), was the grandson of a Great Yarmouth man.

John Mason, born at King's Lynn in 1586, was the founder of New Hampshire. He published the first reliable maps of the area and later became its governor. He returned to Britain in later life and is buried in Westminster Abbey.

ARTS & LITERATURE

Sixteen Revelations of Divine Love (1393) by Mother Julian of Norwich, was the first book to be written by a woman in English.

Margery Kempe, born at King's Lynn in 1373, wrote *The Book of Margery Kempe,* the first known autobiography in English literature.

The formidable Margaret Paston (born Margaret Mauteby at Reedham in 1421) did not write her letters for public consumption, but when they were discovered 300 years later at Oxnead Hall (along with correspondence from her husband John and other family members) their contents revealed the greatest insight into the private lives of English gentry during the Wars of the Roses and were duly published.

George Henry Borrow, author of *The Bible in Spain*, *Lavengro* and *Romany Rye* was born at East Dereham on 5 July 1803.

Edward Seago, born in Norwich in 1910, was a self-taught artist whose watercolour and oil landscapes received national acclaim. His work was collected by her late Majesty Queen Elizabeth, the Queen Mother. Ted Seago's paintings were published in a number of books that reflected the travels and experiences of the author, among them are: *Circus Company* (1933); *The Country Scene* (1936) containing forty-two paintings accompanying John Masefield's poetry; *Caravan*

(1937); *Peace in War* (1943); *High Endeavour* (1944); *Tideline* (1948) and *With Capricorn to Paris* (1956).

Richard Porson was born at East Ruston on Christmas Day in 1759. His family were poor but the boy showed great promise, even genius, and with help from the local curate, the Revd Hewitt, and John Norris of Witton Park, Porson was sent to Eton and progressed to Trinity College, Cambridge. He went on to be appointed Regius Professor of Greek and edited what became regarded as the definitive editions of many Greek plays.

Henry Rider Haggard (1856–1925), the author of such epic adventures as *King Solomon's Mines* and *She*, was born at Bradenham near East Dereham and spent some of his later life at Ditchingham.

Norwich-born Mary Mann (1848–1929) was a prolific Victorian novelist whose career spanned thirty-five years. Moving to Shropham after her marriage, she set many of her fictional stories in the county and drew inspiration from what she saw around her. Although her stories were fictional, her depiction of the hardships of country folk was only too real. Described by some as 'Norfolk's Thomas Hardy', Mann was much-admired by D.H. Lawrence. Her books include *The Parish of Hilby* (1883) and *The Fields of Dulditch* (1902).

The nautical novelist Captain Frederick Marryat (1792–1848), the creator of *Mr Midshipman Easy* (1836), spent his latter years at Langham where he wrote *Children of the New Forest* (1847).

Amelia Opie (1771–1853), socialite, novelist and poet, and known as 'The Gay Quaker', was born in Norwich in 1771. Her first novel *The Dangers of Coquetry* was published when she was just eighteen. Amelia is buried in the Gildencroft Quaker Cemetery, Norwich.

William Crotch (1775–1847), musical child prodigy who played before George III aged three-and-a-half and went on to be appointed Professor of Music at St John's College, Oxford, where he taught for fifty years, was born at Norwich.

Celebrated nineteenth-century violinist Antonio Oury lived out his last years in Norfolk and died at East Dereham on 25 July 1883.

Alfred Stannard, the last survivor of the Norwich School of Artists commenced with old Crome, died on 26 January 1889 at St Andrew's Hall Plain, Norwich, in his eighty-third year.

Sir Alfred Munnings, one of England's finest painters of horses, was born just over the border at Mendham in Suffolk and moved to Norwich aged fourteen to take up a position as apprentice to Page Brothers, the Norwich lithographers, creating posters and advertisements, and studied at the Norwich School of Art in the evenings. Some of Munnings' earliest commissions came from Shaw Tomkins, manager of Caley's and one of Page Brothers' most important customers, who commissioned Munnings to design posters and boxes for chocolates.

Luke Hansard, the man who printed the *Journals of the House of Commons* from 1774 until his death in 1828, and whose legacy remains in the name of the record of parliamentary debate, was born in St Mary's parish, Norwich, in 1752.

Ralph Hale Mottram (1883–1971), novelist and local historian, was born in Norwich and was, for many years, the literary doyen of the city. He is best remembered for his Spanish Farm Trilogy (1927) based on his experiences as a young officer on the Western Front during the First World War. The trilogy comprised *The Spanish Farm*, *Sixty-Four, Ninety-Four* and *The Crime at Vanderlynden's*; it was later made into a film called the *Roses of Picardy*.

The Revd Samuel F. Leighton Green MC and Bar (1882–1929), the author of *The Happy Padre*, an account of his experiences as a military chaplain on the Western Front, was Rector of St Barnabas's Church, Heigham, before and immediately after the First World War until he was appointed Rector of All Saints' Church, Mundesley. He died as incumbent of that role and was buried with full military honours in the churchyard.

Mrs Rose Ellen Thackeray, widow of the Rector of Horstead and Coltishall, was the author of *Social Skeletons* and *Pictures of the Past*, and also a regular contributor of poetical sketches to various magazines in the nineteenth century. She died in her seventy-ninth year on 23 January 1889 while residing in Great Yarmouth.

Augustus Jessopp, academic, antiquarian and author of a number of volumes including *The Coming of the Friars*, *Arcady for Better or Worse* and *The Trials of a Country Parson,* was headmaster of King Edward VI School in Norwich and Rector of Scarning for thirty-two years. He will probably be best remembered, however, for his published description of an encounter with a ghost at Mannington Hall in 1879.

Robert Ladbrooke, artist and engraver who artistically and loyally captured much of Norfolk in the first half of the nineteenth century, died at his home on Scole's Green, Norwich, on 11 October 1842 aged seventy-three.

Wilkie Collins (1824–89) visited Winterton in 1864 while researching his novel *Armadale* (1866) and fell in love with a local girl Martha Rudd when she was nineteen and he was forty. Martha later returned to London with him where they lived as husband and wife under the name Mr and Mrs William Dawson and had three children together.

War Poet Siegfried Sassoon spent a number of childhood holidays with his mother and brothers at the Old Rectory in Edingthorpe and visited the village again after the First World War. Sassoon recorded his reminiscences of the village and district in his autobiography *The Old Century and Seven More Years* (1938) and again in *The Flower Show Match and Other Pieces* (1941).

Agatha Christie frequently stayed with her friends the McLeods at their home 'The Shrubbery' on Cromer Road, North Walsham, and even wrote some of her books while she stayed there. Some of the characters she included were based on local people she encountered during her visits.

Frankfort Manor, now known as Sloley Old Hall, was rented by Sylvia Townsend Warner – author of *Lolly Willowes* (1926), *Mr Fortune's Maggot* (1927), *The True Heart* and *Summer Will Show* (1936), *After The Death of Don Juan* (1938), *The Corner That Held Them* (1948) and *The Flint Anchor* (1954) – with her lover the poet Valentine Ackland between May 1933 and 1934. Both women were active in the Communist Party of Great Britain, and visited Spain during the Civil War.

Doreen Rash of Diss, a fearless anti-tithe campaigner described as 'a latter-day Boadicea' published over fifty books under the pen name of Doreen Wallace.

Despite having no previous experience of farming, Henry Williamson, the author of *Tarka the Otter*, purchased Old Hall Farm, Stiffkey, in 1937 and wrote *The Story of a Norfolk Farm* (1941) about his experiences.

Edward Bickersteth was born at Banningham Rectory on 26 June 1850. Son of a noted ecclesiastical family, his father was the Bishop of Exeter from 1885 to 1900. Edward also became a man of the cloth and became the missionary Bishop of South Tokyo. He died in post in 1897. Mourned not only in England but also in his missionary centres at Delhi and Tokyo, his story was told in *The Life and Letters of Edward Bickersteth* by Samuel Bickersteth (his son) published in 1899.

As a young man, poet Stephen Spender (1909–95) spent many happy holidays with his family at the house they leased at Sheringham called 'The Bluff'.

Playwright and novelist Patrick Hamilton (1904–62), the author of such novels as *Twenty Thousand Streets Under the Sky* (1935), *Impromtu in Morbundia* (1939), *Hangover Square* (1941) and *The Slaves of Solitude* (1947), spent his later life at Sheringham and his ashes were scattered at Blakeney.

Sidney Grapes (1888–1958) of Potter Heigham wrote his 'Boy John' letters, consisting of local anecdotes and wisdom written in the broad Norfolk dialect to the *Eastern Daily Press* between 1946 and 1958. Collected and published in book form, his works remain well-loved to this day.

Captain W.E. Johns, the creator of 'Biggles', lived and worked as a Sanitary Inspector in Swaffham before the First World War. He joined his first military unit there in 1913, the local troop of the Norfolk Yeomanry and later served with the unit in Gallipoli. On 6 October 1914 Johns married Maude Penelope Hunt (1882–1961), the daughter of the Revd John Hunt, the vicar at Little Dunham in Norfolk.

Sir John Mills was born at the Watt's Naval Training School, North Elmham, in 1908 and was educated at the Norwich High School for Boys (now Langley School). He also had football trials with Norwich City in the 1920s before moving into acting.

Affectionately remembered television children's entertainer Richard Hearne, better known as 'Mr Pastry', was born on Lady Lane in Norwich in 1908.

Sir Michael Caine (born Maurice Joseph Micklewhite) was evacuated to North Runcton in Norfolk during the Second Wold War.

Philip Pullman, best known as the best-selling author of the His Dark Materials trilogy of fantasy novels, was born in Norwich on 19 October 1946.

Roger Taylor, drummer with the rock band Queen, was born at King's Lynn in 1949.

Martin Brundle, former racing driver, was born in King's Lynn in 1959, as was his son Alex in 1990, who has followed in his father's footsteps as a racing driver.

Matt Smith, actor and eleventh incarnation of Doctor Who, studied drama at the University of East Anglia.

Terry Molloy, the actor who played Davros, creator of the Daleks in *Dr Who*, lives at Bawburgh. Terry has also played Mike Tucker on BBC Radio 4's *The Archers* since 1973.

Tim Westwood, BBC Radio 1 rap DJ and presenter of popular MTV show *Pimp My Ride (UK)* grew up in and around Norwich.

Norfolk Coast is the fifteenth studio album by The Stranglers.

Norfolk Rhapsodies Nos 1 and 2 were composed by Ralph Vaughan Williams. He visited Norfolk on a number of occasions and wrote his *Sea Symphony* while staying at Martincross in Sheringham in 1919.

In his 1971 classic *Life on Mars* David Bowie mentions the Norfolk Broads.

SHERLOCK HOLMES & NORFOLK

Sir Arthur Conan Doyle, the creator of the great fictional detective Sherlock Holmes, knew north-east Norfolk well and visited on a number of occasions. In *The Adventure of the Dancing Men* (1903) Holmes arrives at North Walsham station and travels to Ridling Thorpe Manor to crack a crime by deciphering a code composed of dancing stick men; a story inspired by the real-life unusual code that Doyle saw used by the son of the owner of the Hill House pub in Happisburgh. People who know this area well will also notice a number of our distinctive local surnames and place name amalgams in this book and others by Doyle. It is also believed his creation of the *Hound of the Baskervilles* is based, at least in part, on the tales he heard of our own devil dog 'Black Shuck' when Doyle was staying the county in 1901. He also visited Cromer Hall, an edifice that certainly bears a strong resemblance to his description of Baskerville Hall.

THREE LOST STARS OF FOLK

Sam Larner was born at Winterton in 1878. He first went to sea at the age of eight and spent most of his working life as a fisherman, developing his repertoire and style from the locality and his workmates. He was discovered in 1956 and his album *Now is the Time for Fishing* was originally recorded on location in 1958–60 by Ewan MacColl and Peggy Seeger and released in 1961. This record has come to be regarded as one of the most important recordings of an English traditional singer ever made. Ewan MacColl went on to write the book *The Shoals of Herring*, based on Larner's life. Sam passed away in 1965 but his songs are still loved to this day.

Folk singer Walter Pardon was born at Knapton in 1914. He was a quiet man who disliked publicity, preferring small gatherings to perform his songs and he was happiest when sharing them with younger singers. He drew international interest after an album of his *Bright Golden Store* of songs (that was how he referred to his repertoire, it was also the name of the album) was released in 1984. Walter appeared as far afield as the Smithsonian Institution in Washington where he was invited to take part in the bicentennial celebrations in 1976 and he was presented with a Gold Badge by the English Folk Dance & Song Society in 1983. He passed away on 9 June 1996.

Folk singer Peter Bellamy (1944–91), a founding member of the Young Tradition, spent his formative years living in the village of Warham and attended Fakenham Grammar School. Bellamy did much to promote and preserve the folk music of Norfolk and his LPs include *Mainly Norfolk* (1968), *Fair England's Shore* (1968), *The Fox Jumped Over The Parson's Gate* (1969), *Oak Ash and Thorn* (1970), *Won't You Go My Way* (1971) and *Barrack Room Ballads of Rudyard Kipling* (1975). Pete wrote the ballad-opera *The Transports* in 1973 and it took him four years to find a company willing to produce it in 1977 – it then became the folk record of the year.

5

NORFOLK AT WORK

INVENTIONS & INNOVATIONS

Anthony de Solempne, a 'Stranger' refugee from Brabant in the southern Netherlands, was the first Norwich printer. He arrived in 1567 and established his business at the Sign of the White Dove, later at the Edinburgh Arms on Dove Street.

In February 1878 experiments with telephones were made in the counting house of J. and J. Colman, Carrow Works, Norwich, under the direction of Mr H. Sack, superintendent of the Great Eastern Railway telegraph department. Telephones were attached to Colman's private wires to London via Ipswich and the railway company's wires via Cambridge to London Liverpool Street. Parties of ladies and gentlemen at both ends were distinctly heard and they were able to converse but it was concluded, 'it does not appear that at present the telephone can be adapted to public use.'

CARROW WORKS, NORWICH.

The first person in Norwich to advertise patent photographic portraits was Mr Beard of the Royal Bazaar in December 1843 with prices ranging from 1 to 2 guineas.

George Allen of St Stephen's was the first to introduce the manufacture of elastic cloth to Norwich in November 1860.

Ben Elder is the Norwich dyer first credited in 1759 with the 'Norwich Red' dye for which its fancy, vivid fabrics were renowned.

In December 1864 it was announced that Thomas W. Rutland, carpenter of West Wymer Street in Norwich, had invented a communication cord by which means passengers could communicate with both driver and guard, and at the same time a signal would be exhibited to indicate from which carriage the alarm was given.

England's first provincial newspaper was the *Norwich Post*, first printed in the city in 1701 by Francis Burges. The city also holds the record for the longest continuously printed local newspaper, the *Norwich Mercury*, founded in 1714.The *Eastern Daily Press* is a comparative latecomer with its first edition being published on 10 October 1870.

The inventor of perforated postage stamps was Yarmouth man Charles Crawshay Wilkinson, who died in the town in March 1881.

One of the first fire escapes was invented by the Revd Mr Arthy of Caistor near Norwich in 1836, and the very first fire escape designed for the evacuation of populous buildings was invented by Captain Longe of Spixworth Park in 1886.

The first direct communication between Norwich and London was made through the electric telegraph on 9 July 1846.

Never wasteful – when Staff and Chamberlin chandlers of St Martin-at-Palace, Norwich, was destroyed by fire in October 1822, several hogsheads of tallow melted and ran down the streets and into the river. Local folk went out in their boats and skimmed off at least 10cwt of tallow for their own use.

During the 1930s Herbert Rumsey Wells, creator and manufacturer of the 'Doggie cap' at his premises on St Andrew's Street, Norwich, proudly claimed to be 'the most expensive capmaker in the world'.

SIX NOTABLE NORFOLK BUSINESSES

Colman's of Norwich can trace is roots back to 1814 when flour miller Jeremiah James Colman took over a mustard manufacturing business at Stoke Holy Cross. Jeremiah took his adopted nephew James into partnership in 1823 and the firm of J & J Colman was created. The business grew and acquired larger premises at Carrow in 1856 where new, more efficient production methods were introduced. The Colmans were also benevolent, building a subsidised school for the children of their employees in 1857, and they also appointed one of the very first industrial nurses and even established one of the first works canteens in the city. Realising the importance of product visibility, they introduced very distinctive mustard yellow packaging in 1866 and that same year were granted a special warrant as Manufacturers to Her Majesty Queen Victoria. By the early twentieth century Colman's employed over 3,000 Norwich citizens in mustard, starch and corn flour production. The Colman's brand was purchased by Unilever in 1995.

Jarrold's was founded in 1770 as drapers and grocers in Woodbridge, Suffolk, and expanded into printing in 1815. Taking over their first premises in Norwich in 1823 to sell books and stationery, they moved the printing business to the same site in 1830. A nineteenth-century advert states they were 'printers, binders, fancy stationers, die sinkers and engravers' and they maintain a fine reputation for printing at their works in the historic St James Mill to this day. Occupying part of their present site as early as 1840, the present department store in Norwich was designed by George Skipper and built between 1903 and 1905. The Jarrold stores, always synonymous with a touch of class and good quality, remain in family hands.

Lotus Cars was established by Colin Chapman in some old stables behind the Railway Hotel, Hornsey, North London, in 1952. The business went from strength to strength, first moving to a purpose-built factory at Cheshunt in 1959, then to a modern factory and road test facility at Hethel in 1966. Lotus continues to design and build their unique sports and racing cars, renowned for their light weight and fine handling characteristics, on the site.

British Sugar at Cantley is a landmark that is visible for miles around. Built in 1912, it became the first British sugar factory and still produces sugar of various kinds and animal feed during the annual harvesting season. Today, it is one of the last remaining British Sugar factories left in the country (the others are Newark-on-Trent, Bury St Edmunds and Wissington).

Norwich Union was founded in 1797 in Norwich, when merchant and banker Thomas Bignold formed the Norwich Union Society for

the Insurance of Houses, Stock and Merchandise from Fire, later known as the Norwich Union Fire Insurance Office. After a severe winter that caused widespread suffering and loss of life, Bignold founded the Norwich Union Life Insurance Society in 1808. By the early twentieth century Norwich Union societies were operating worldwide and in 1925 the two Norwich Union companies were brought together when the Life Society bought the entire share capital of the Fire Society. After a number of mergers Norwich Union is now part of the Aviva Group.

Bernard Matthews began his business from his own home with twenty turkey eggs and a second-hand incubator in 1950. The business began to grow but suffered a great setback when almost all the sheds he had built for his birds were destroyed in the high winds of 1953. Needing more solid premises, Bernard and his wife Joyce bought the dilapidated Great Witchingham Hall for £3,000 in 1955. Bernard filled most of the hall's rooms with turkeys; hatching and rearing the birds in the bedrooms and preparing them in the hall kitchen, while he and his wife lived in two unheated rooms. The couple worked long hours and the business really took off as the freezer revolution transformed the demand for oven-ready turkeys. In 1980 Bernard fronted the first TV commercial for turkey breast roast with his comment 'Bootiful', and Bernard Matthews turkeys became a household name.

SOME SIGNIFICANT NORFOLK
INDUSTRIES OF THE PAST

Norfolk Wool and Weaving

Wool was big business in medieval England. There was enormous demand for it, mainly to produce cloth and everyone who had land – from peasants to major landowners such as the religious houses – raised sheep. Wool became the backbone and driving force of the medieval English economy between the late thirteenth and late fifteenth centuries. The trade was described as 'the jewel in the realm' and Norfolk truly had the golden fleece as demonstrated by the great number of churches in the county built and endowed from the profits of wool and weaving. The most popular yarn and cloth of the age was Worsted and it takes its name from the village in our county (the village named is now spelt Worstead) a centre of production of the cloth from the twelfth century, along with North Walsham and Aylsham.

Norwich Shawls

Alderman John Harvey is credited with the introduction of shawl manufacture in Norwich in the 1780s (though some sources quote yarn factor Mr Edward Barrow was the first man to manufacture cotton and shawls in the city). The heyday of Norwich shawls was in the 1840 and '50s. There were at least twenty-eight manufacturers producing shawls in the city at this time. One firm, E.&F. Hinde, made no less than twenty-six different types of shawl, representing a total of 39,000 shawls for one year. Norwich shawls were always highly prized for their bright colours and fine designs but the trade was not to last forever and by the 1860s they were fast falling out of fashion. Only a few firms manufacturing shawls in the city survived into the twentieth century.

Norwich Boot and Shoe Trade

As the cloth manufacturing industry declined in Norwich during the nineteenth century, boot and shoe manufacture ascended as one of the major employers. Increasing competition from American imports in the latter half of the nineteenth century saw the greater part of the shoe manufacturing industry invest heavily in the construction of imposing and impressive 'super factories' in order to compete. This investment was often made possible by the larger, successful firms amalgamating, thus many firms have names such as Sexton, Son &

Now Showing in the Shops

MASCOT 2045.—A smart shoe in choice of Patent, Black or Coloured Glace Kids, with insertion - - **21/-**

MASCOT 1841.—Dainty Court shoe in Patent, Black or Coloured Glace Kids - **21/-**

NORVIC MASCOT

Every well-dressed woman will need a copy of the handsome NORVIC & MASCOT Booklet, illustrating over 100 Styles of Fashion and Charm—Post Free.

NORVIC SHOE CO., NORWICH

Everard, or Howlett & White. In the early twentieth century shoe manufacture in Norwich was at its zenith employing upwards of 12,000 personnel. A number of brand names stand out as household names: Howlett & White's 'Norvic' Shoes and James Southall & Co's Start-Rite shoes for children. The great British shoe manufacturing industry gradually died over the latter half of the twentieth century as cheap imports made it impossible for home-grown firms to compete. One by one most of the super factories closed down, leaving just a few British manufacturers of premium quality footwear today.

Caley's

A.J. Caley established himself as a chemist on London Street in Norwich in 1857. He began making mineral waters in his cellar in 1863, the business took off and moved to larger premises on London Street. Caley's son Edward joined the business in 1878 and they took over their first building on Chapelfield. In 1883 Caley's began manufacturing cocoa and went from strength to strength, enjoying patronage from both the royal family and the House of Commons. Caley's erected a purpose-built factory, became a joint stock company in 1890 and started making crackers in 1897. The business remained in the hands of the Caley family until 1918, when it was purchased by the African and Eastern Trade Corporation who sold the firm to John Mackintosh & Sons Limited, 'The Yorkshire Toffee King', for £138,000 in 1932. After further takeover by Rowntree and finally

Nestlé, the chocolate factory that filled the city air with its warm and tempting smell was closed in 1994 and the Chapelfield shopping mall has been built in its place. The Caley name has been revived by a smaller company which still maintains the best traditions of Caley chocolates. Yummy.

Campbell's Soups

Campbell's was a landmark business in the county, literally – its tower can be seen for miles around the King's Lynn area. This was the first major Campbell's factory outside the USA with the first cans rolling off the production line here in 1959. By 1979 the business was employing more than 500 staff and making 60 varieties of soup. The company was bought out in 1996 and the site was closed in 2007 with the loss of 245 jobs.

Wincarnis

Originally called Liebig's Extract of Meat and Malt Wine, the tonic wine was first produced under the brand name of Wincarnis by Coleman and Co. Ltd at Norwich in 1887. The product took off and the Wincarnis Works on Westwick Street produced and sent the product all over the world.

The Norwich Brewing Industry

Brewing in Norwich can be traced back centuries. During the eighteenth century larger-scale breweries began to emerge and by 1836 twenty-seven breweries were recorded in the city. When the railway arrived in Norwich the brewing industry really flourished as the breweries were able to send their wares across the county and further afield. By the 1920s four big breweries dominated the business in Norwich, they were: Morgans, Steward & Patteson, Youngs Crawshay & Youngs and Bullard's. Further takeovers forced the demise of brewing in Norwich when the last breweries came under the control of just one company, Watney Mann, in the 1970s. Small-scale independent brewing continues in Norwich but there are no large breweries left in the city today.

Hobbies of Dereham

Started by Mr J.H. Skinner in East Dereham in 1897, the business rapidly grew to occupy a large works in the town manufacturing fretwork machines and kits that were exported all over the world. The business was subject to a number of takeovers and finally closed in 1977. The trade name and trademarks of Hobbies continue as a mail order supplier for model makers with a shop at Raveningham.

Cranes of Dereham

The business began when William Crane established a blacksmith's shop at Great Fransham in 1865. A man keen to progress, by the 1880s William was advertising his business as an agricultural implement maker, joiner, builder, smith, wheelwright and church bell-hanger. William passed away in 1906 and his two sons carried on the business acquiring Mallon's agricultural engineers at South Green in East Dereham in 1913. Incorporated in 1920 as Crane (Dereham) Ltd, the business expanded in the 1920s and '30s by making drawbar trailers. Cranes became a public company in 1950 and expanded again in 1960, setting up a factory for semi-trailers at North Walsham. The following year the company became joint venture Crane Fruehauf Trailers Ltd. The 1960s were good for the business; the company grew, developed new factories, adapted with the changing requirements of the industry by producing a good range from dry freight, insulated and refrigerated trailers to low-loaders, tippers, hopper and tanker trailers, and they also acquired other companies. But after more takeovers in the 1990s the business declined, contracted and closed in 2005.

Barnards Ltd, Norwich

Charles Barnard began as an ironmonger, oil and colourman in Norwich in 1826 and entered into a partnership with John Bishop in 1846. Their business grew and soon they occupied premises in St George's Street and Coslany Street. The business moved again to St Michael's Coslany where they erected the Norfolk Iron Works. The company made its name inventing and manufacturing the original galvanised wire netting and slow combustion stoves. Their reputation, however, was made on their vast range of wrought and cast iron products, especially fireplaces, and obtained a royal warrant as makers of iron gates and railings 'By Appointment' to both King George V and King George VI and provided many supplies for the military in both world wars. Barnards developed their business to a factory on Mousehold from the 1920s, where they concentrated on the production of wire fencing products from the 1950s but after a number of takeovers the business finally closed its doors in Norwich in 1991.

Brush Making at Wymondham

Wymondham has a long tradition of wood working; a spoon and spigot even appear on the town's coat of arms. Brush making had been carried out in the town since the nineteenth century but after the Briton Brush Company was formed with the amalgamation of S.D. Page & Son and Matthew's of Tottenham, the new company extended and developed the factory on Lady Lane into one of the most up-to-date brush factories in the country, with its own railway sidings, saw mills, and engineering workshops. The factory took in English trees and other raw materials and produced complete and finished brushware that was exported all over the

world. In its heyday the factory employed over 600 staff. Times changed in the later twentieth century and cheap imports sounded the death knell for the brush industry. The Wymondham brush factory closed in 1985 and the site is now occupied by a housing estate.

Boulton & Paul

Established Norwich ironmonger and foundry owner William Staples Boulton made his manager Mr J.J. Dawson Paul a partner in the business in 1869 and renamed the firm Boulton & Paul. At their Rose Lane Works they made all manner of iron products, from hand implements and fencing to iron building furniture. By 1900 the firm had expanded to further premises on King Street and were supplying their products all over the world. Their greatest challenge came during the First World War when the government asked them to start making aeroplanes. Constructing an airfield on the old cavalry drill ground on Mousehold Heath, their first aircraft was completed and awaiting its test in October 1915. Boulton & Paul had built 2,530 military aircraft by the end of the war. The pressures of war production saw Boulton & Paul move to a 14-acre site soon known as Riverside Works. After the war, B&P were awarded the contract to construct parts for the R101 airship. These parts were manufactured at Norwich then sent to the airship base at Cardington for assembly. During the Second World War, B&P works in Norwich produced a huge variety of items, from Morrison air raid shelters to tank transporters and noses for Horsa gliders. Despite being bombed on more than one occasion they carried on. By the 1980s B&P was in decline and the Riverside Works closed in 1986, was demolished, and the site is now occupied by the Riverside shopping, leisure and residential area.

THEY KEPT A' TROSHIN'

It was recorded in March 1825 that farm labourer James Catchpole of Shelfanger was willing and able to do a day's work on the land, even though he was in his 105th year.

In July 1803 bricklayer William Green accepted a wager of 5 guineas he could not lay 3,800 bricks in a workmanlike manner in 24 hours. His work, on the new bowling green house, was completed in just 20 hours.

When Mrs Phoebe Crew of St George's, Tombland, Norwich, passed away aged seventy-seven, she had served forty years' practice as a midwife. Over that time she brought 9,730 babies into the world.

John Cubitt, the last true Worsted weaver of Worstead, died in the village in 1882 aged ninety-one.

Thomas Row, the last of the Binham wool combers, and indeed the last of a trade that dated back hundreds of years in the village, died in April 1838 aged eighty-nine.

Swanton Abbot was home to Jimmy Davison, Norfolk's 'King of the Mole Catchers'. Many tales grew up around this character in the 1920s and '30s. He was liked by children, he always had time for a yarn and would show the moles, saying they were, in fact, fairy princesses in fur coats. He would also net sparrows (they were common enough at the time to be pests to farmers). These little birds would not be wasted; they would be made into the local delicacy of sparrow pie.

Matthew Joy 'The Walking Baker' died in June 1823. For the last eleven years of his life he had carried his large basket of bread, weighing around 8 stones, about his shoulders to make his deliveries to outlying villages around Norwich – a journey of about 20 miles a day. It was calculated that over that time he had walked about 68,440 miles.

Robert Maidstone served Great Plumstead for more than fifty years as parish clerk but rather than completely retire, he spent the last twenty years of his life, until his death aged 100 in May 1871, as the village postmaster.

Jack Gedge (1886–1986) was the last old Norfolk wherryman. Born at Worstead, he was the third generation of his family to work on the Broads.

6

FARMING TIMES

'TURNIP' TOWNSHEND

Charles Townshend, 2nd Viscount Townshend of Raynham Hall (18 April 1674–21 June 1738) was known as 'Turnip' Townshend because of his great interest in farming and agricultural improvement. Responsible for the introduction of large-scale turnip cultivation into England, Townshend also promoted four-field crop rotation of wheat, barley, a root crop and clover, a system (pioneered by farmers in the Waasland region of Flanders) that proved to be a key development in the British Agricultural Revolution. Norfolk four-course crop rotation provided a fodder crop and grazing crop that allowed livestock to be bred all year round, brought fields that would have been left fallow for a year into use, and helped prevent the build-up of crop-specific soil pests and diseases.

MILESTONES ON THE LAND

A machine for removing lice from peas was exhibited by Mr Paul of Startson in 1807. Two men working the contraption for four hours removed 24 pecks of lice.

In August 1807 Edmund Reader of Sisland near Loddon took a bet of 5 guineas that he could cut (by scythe) and tie 1 acre of wheat in 16 hours. Performing the feat in Mr Burton's field at Barford, Reader cut 1 acre and 7 roods and had tied 430 sheaves.

An annual ploughing match to encourage the use of oxen in farming was inaugurated at Ellingham in 1808 by the Revd William Johnson.

Brilliant arithmetician John Cullyer, the author of *The Gentleman's and Farmer's Assistant*, died at Wymondham aged eighty-one in 1844

In a groundbreaking experiment, tobacco was grown in the Feltwell area in the early twentieth century.

Industrial-scale sugar beet production was introduced to Norfolk from Holland in 1912.

The first modern union for agricultural labourers, the Eastern Counties Agricultural Labourers' and Smallholders' Union, was founded by the great campaigner George Edwards at an inaugural meeting held at the Angel Inn, North Walsham, on 20 July 1906.

COKE OF HOLKHAM

Thomas William Coke, 1st Earl of Leicester (6 May 1754–30 June 1842), known as Coke of Norfolk, was a British politician and agricultural reformer. Coke's greatest contribution to agriculture improvements came in two areas – grasses and husbandry. He pioneered the use of cocksfoot and lucerne as grass and feed respectively. He championed innovation in agriculture by instigating the Holkham Sheep Shearings, foreshadowing the county shows of today, where experts on all aspects of farming could meet with farmers from across the county and beyond to discuss and demonstrate the latest methods of food production and animal husbandry.

THE ROYAL NORFOLK SHOW

The Norfolk Agricultural Association was formed from the amalgamation of the East Norfolk and West Norfolk Agricultural Associations in 1847 and held its first show on the Norwich Cricket Ground the same year.

For the first fifteen years the newly formed Norfolk Agricultural Association Shows alternated between Norwich and Swaffham.

From 1862 until 1953 shows were held throughout the county with the cooperation and support of landowners with parkland sites.

There were no shows in 1866, 1911, 1934 and 1957 when the Royal Show was held locally and the Norfolk Show was amalgamated with

that event. The 1866 show was cancelled because of Cattle Plague and the 2001 show was cancelled owing to the outbreak of Foot and Mouth Disease. No summer shows were held during the war years 1914–18 and 1940–5.

In 1908 the asociation was granted the great privilege of the 'Royal' prefix by King Edward VII.

The Royal Norfolk Agricultural Association made its initial purchase of land at Costessey for its permanent showground in 1952 and the first show was staged on the site in 1954.

Today, the Royal Norfolk Show is the largest two-day agricultural show in the country.

THE COUNTY LORE OF THE FARM LABOURERS' WORKING DAY

Traditionally, the labourer begins work at sun up, and concludes his labours by sun down.

Every day was interspersed with breaks otherwise described as 'whets' or 'naps'.

The day would start with the dew drink, often just cold tea or spring water. Few would have had a hearty breakfast, and indeed most would have regularly started their day with just bread and cheese, perhaps a boiled egg or a bit of bacon for a treat.

As the sun gets high in the sky the labourer knows it's time for 'levenses and a good drink from the bottle of cold tea he had brought with him. This would be only a brief break and if the labourer had been standing to do his task he may well not sit down lest he 'get stuck' (get tempted to linger too long over his break) and then back to work until lunch time.

Lunch break was known as 'noonins' and the workman would stop for a while and walk to a bank, probably shaded by a tree or hedge, or haystack and sit down with his workmates. The real old labourers were known to chew tobacco and would take the chunk from their mouth and if they were bald they would remove their hats, stick the sticky chewed 'baccy' on the top of their head, put their hat back on and have their lunch. This repast would usually consist of a hunk of bread, a bit of cheese, an onion and perhaps an apple or a pear if in season. During 'noonins', life, country philosophy, jokes, local sports and 'wass gorn on in the village' would be discussed. Then off to work again for the afternoon; many of the men puffing away determinedly on their roll-up fags as they walked back.

'Fourses' was the last break, usually about four in the afternoon, hence the name. The wife of the labourer might bring or send one of the children over ready for this break with a billycan of milk 'sop' – milk with bread 'bobs' broken into it, sometimes heated up. If it was harvest time or the men deserved reward, the farmer might well send over a flagon of beer in a stone jar encased in a handled wicker basket.

SOME OLD NORFOLK FRUIT VARIETIES

Oxnead Pearmain
Norwich White Pippin
Downham Pippin
Britannia Pear
Colonel Harbord's Pippin
Norfolk Colman
Fouldon Pearmain

Norfolk Beefin' Apple
Ringwood's Seedling
Hethersett Pippin
St Augustine's Grape
The Caroline
Horsham Russet
Vicar of Beighton

COUNTING SHEEP

In order to keep an accurate account of the likes of births or deaths, or to detect strays, shepherds performed frequent head-counts of their flocks. Rather than counting with conventional numbers as we know them today, shepherds had their own numbering system. They would vary from region to region; this one was recorded as being in use in West Norfolk in the nineteenth century:

Yan (1), Tan (2), Tethera (3), Pethera (4), Pip (5), Sethera (6), Lethera (7), Hovera (8), Covera (9), Dick (10), Yan-a-dick (11), Tan-a-dick (12), Thethera-dick (13), Pethera-dick (14), Bumfit (15), Yan-a-bum (16), Tan-a-bum (17), Thether-a-bum (18), Mether-a-bum (19), Jigget (20).

The number system stopped at number twenty; the shepherd would then make a mark on a piece of stick and then count another twenty, and so on.

7

THAT'S ENTERTAINMENT

IT HAPPENED HERE

The greatest violinist of his day, Niccolò Paganini, performed at the Corn Exchange, Norwich, on 28 and 29 July 1829 and at the Theatre on 30 July. He was curiously described in the local press as a 'fascinating, but by no means fair-dealing, foreigner.'

Virtuoso pianist and composer Franz Lizst played concerts at the Assembly Rooms and the Theatre at Norwich in September 1840.

Pablo Fanque (born William Derby), the first black circus proprietor in Britain, was born in Norwich in 1796. Some of the entertainers 'late of Pablo Fanque's Fair' are mentioned in the Beatles song on 'Being For the Benefit of Mr. Kite' on their *Sergeant Pepper* album after John Lennon was inspired by an old bill poster advertisement for their show.

In December 1863 an act consisting of a man and a woman, said to be Kaffirs, who fed upon live rats in the presence of continually succeeding audiences, caused public disgust at Wells Fair. Upon being made aware of the exhibition's vile content, the police expelled the performers from the town.

The phonograph described as 'Edison's wonderful talking machine' was exhibited for the first time in Norwich by Mr William Lynd M.I.C.E. on 26 April 1889.

Barnum & Bailey's 'Greatest Show on Earth' came to Norwich in September 1898. Located on a piece of land on Unthank Road, upwards of 42,000 people visited the show over two days.

Founded by and very much the vision of Nugent Monck, the Maddermarket Theatre opened in 1921 was the first permanent recreation of an Elizabethan Theatre in Britain.

The West Runton Pavilion hosted T. Rex, Black Sabbath, AC/DC, the Jam, the Clash, Def Leppard, Dire Straits and Duran Duran.

The Beatles performed at the Grosvenor Rooms in Norwich on 17 May 1963.

Jimi Hendrix played the Orford Cellar at Norwich on 25 January 1967.

The Sex Pistols played their penultimate UK gig at Links Pavilion, Cromer, on 24 December 1977.

I LIKE A CHALLENGE . . .

Comic actor and dancer Will Kempe danced the Morris from the Mansion House, London, to the churchyard of St Peter Mancroft, Norwich. He called the journey his 'Nine Days Wonder' and he travelled on nine days spread out over four weeks during February and March 1599.

In 1826 Mr Gibson accepted a wager of £50 to walk from Norwich to Yarmouth in 7½ hours carrying £4 worth of copper coins, weighing 4 stone 4lb. Starting from Bishop Bridge at 5.00 a.m. he walked the first 12 miles in 3 hours and arrived at Yarmouth half an hour within time.

In 1829 Mary McMullen (aged sixty-one) walked 76 miles in 24 hours on a measured half mile of the Gaywood Road, near King's Lynn. She performed a like feat at North Walsham in March 1830 and crowned off her achievements at Ranelagh Gardens, Norwich, on 26 April 1830 when she walked 100 miles in 24 successive hours.

NINE OUT OF TEN FOR EFFORT . . .

In 1817 Robert Skipper 'The Norwich Pedestrian' took a wager to walk from Norwich to Thetford and back in 12 hours. He walked 54 miles but having only 4 minutes to perform the last mile, gave in. Later that same year he attempted the 60 miles to Dereham and back in 12 hours. He was so exhausted in the last 2 hours that he could not complete his task. In 1818 he wagered he would walk 1,000 miles in 20 successive days. He relinquished his task on the ninth day because he had been struck lame.

BAD REVIEW?

Entertainer Ching Lao Lauro of Drury Lane received what was described as 'the worst review in the history of performance in Norwich' in April 1828. Appearing at Norwich Theatre he performed 'The Man in The Moon' and the newspaper critic did not mince his words: 'no viler tissue of nonsensical stuff could be foisted on the patience of an insulted audience. It had more revolting coarseness and infinitely less ingenuity than ever characterised the worst puppet shows' clumsiest performers.' Lauro fared no better with his second act of 'Harlequin in the Shades' for it: 'descended to the lowest vault of the Capulets, amidst universal hisses which such execrable trash duly called forth, in spite of Ching Lau Lauro swallowing his own head.'

TEN LOST PICTURE HOUSES

Regal, New Road, North Walsham (1931–77)
County, Cawston Road, Aylsham (1937–60)
Picture House, Victoria Road, Diss (1916–73)
Regent, High Street, Downham Market (1932–76)
Coliseum, Gorleston (1913–70)
Regal, Regent Road, Great Yarmouth (1934–88)
Electric Theatre, Broad Street, King's Lynn (1911–38)
Electric Picture Palace, Sheringham (1914–31)
Palace, Guildhall Street, Thetford (1913–84)
Theatre de Luxe, St Andrew's Street, Norwich (1910–57)

SOME RADIO NORFOLK TRIVIA

Radio Norfolk began broadcasting at 5.55 p.m. on 11 September 1980 and the station's first presenter on air was John Mountford.

The station's first home was a former carpet showroom in Norfolk Tower on Surrey Street, Norwich.

The late radio legend Roy Waller worked as an estate agent, at Norwich Union and at the AA before becoming a broadcaster.

Early morning presenter Wally Webb moved to Norfolk when a spell in the Royal Air Force brought him to RAF Coltishall.

David Clayton, the Managing Editor of BBC Radio Norfolk, was a mobile disco DJ in the 1970s who debuted at Costessey Village Hall in 1971 and went on to residencies at the Talk of the East in Norwich and the Ocean Room at Gorleston.

Keith 'Cardboard Shoes' Skues began his broadcasting career on British Forces Network in Cologne, Germany, in 1958. He went on to present on the 'watery wireless' pirate radio station Radio Caroline, then Radio Luxembourg and Radio London and was one of the original presenters on BBC Radio 1 in 1967.

Radio Norfolk was the first BBC local radio station to broadcast in stereo and to cover a whole county.

ANGLIA TELEVISION TRIVIA TREASURES

Anglia Television first went on air on 27 October 1959.

Anglia's first newsreaders were 'Sandy' Newman Sanders, Drew Russell and Colin Bower.

Anglia's flagship nature documentary series *Survival* was first broadcast in 1961 and ran to over 900 episodes. The distinguished narrators for the programme over the years included: Orson Welles, Henry Fonda, David Niven, Anthony Hopkins, Robert Powell, Dennis Waterman, Rolf Harris and HRH Prince Philip.

Romper bomper stomper boo. Fondly remembered pre-school children's show Romper Room ran between 1964 and 1977. The presenters were Miss Rosalyn (Rosalyn Thompson 1964–76) and Biddy Massen. Despite reaching the shortlist of six applicants to be the original presenter, Esther Rantzen didn't get the job.

Anglia produced the first version of the show *Mr and Mrs* in 1969 with Norman Vaughan as compère.

'From Norwich – it's The Quiz of the Week . . . *Sale of The Century*' presented by Nicholas Parsons ran between 1971 and 1983. The iconic theme tune 'Joyful Pete' (named so in a gesture to the director Peter Joy) was composed by Peter Fenn, director of music at Anglia, who played live on his organ at every recording.

Another Anglia game show was *Gambit*, based on the card game pontoon hosted by Fred Dineage (1975–82) and Tom O'Connor (1983–5) and featuring Miss Anglia finalist Michelle Lambourne as hostess on almost every episode.

Bygones was presented by affectionately remembered Anglia personality Dick Joice from 1967 until his retirement in 1987.

The famous drawing room introduction scene for each of the Roald Dahl *Tales of the Unexpected* was actually filmed in a specially designed set in a studio at Anglia House.

'BC' the playful leopard cub puppet who 'helped' the *Birthday Club* presenter sort the cards first appeared in 1980.

Anglia shows of the past include: *Contest*, the inter-town quiz hosted by Chris Kelly that aimed to discover which town knows the most about East Anglia; *Farming Diary*, essential Norfolk viewing over the Sunday dinner table; *Craven's Collectables*, John Craven delved into viewers' collections from Beatles memorabilia to Norfolk Regiment militaria; *Weavers Green*, a soap opera based around vets in an East Anglian village launched in 1966 featured early appearances by Wendy Richard and Kate O'Mara; *Backs to the Land*, a sitcom based around Land Girls in the Second World War, made around Heydon in the 1970s; *Timpson's Country Churches* with BBC Radio 4 presenter John Timpson; and *The Warehouse*, a lively blend of comedy, music and the bizarre for young people, featuring cockney comic Lee Hurst.

THE ANGLIA TELEVISION KNIGHT

The Anglia Television knight was used as the company's logo from 1959 to 1988.

The musical fanfare which accompanied each appearance of the rotating knight was a snippet of Handel's 'Water Music' arranged by Sir Malcolm Sargent.

The knight was originally a trophy commissioned by William III of the Netherlands in 1850 for the Falcon Club, a society that met once a year to compete in horse races, falconry and other sports.

The figure and horse are made from a sterling silver. It weighs over 700 troy ounces (22kg, or 48lb) and is modelled on the statue of Richard I that stands outside the Palace of Westminster. It was intended to represent the Black Prince.

The knight was spotted at the Bond Street jewellers, Asprey & Co. and acquired by Anglia Television in 1959.

8

NORFOLK AT PLAY

TEN FACTS ABOUT NORWICH CITY

Norwich City Football Club was formed following a meeting at the Criterion Café in Norwich on 17 June 1902.

Norwich City's song 'On The Ball City' is thought to be the oldest British football chant still being sung today. The song is older than the club itself, having originally been penned for Norwich Teachers or Caley's FC in the 1890s and adapted and adopted by Norwich City in 1902.

The club's original nickname was the Citizens, superseded in 1907 by the more familiar Canaries.

The club played its first regular matches at a ground on Newmarket Road, moving to their first purpose-built ground known as the 'The Nest', constructed on the site of a disused chalk pit on Rosary Road, in 1908. They moved to their current site, Carrow Road, in 1935.

The famous canary badge of Norwich City FC was first adopted in 1922.

Ron Ashman holds the record for Norwich appearances, having played 592 first-team matches between the years 1947 and 1964.

Ralph Hunt holds the record for the most goals scored in a season for Norwich with 31 during the 1955/56 seasons in Division Three (South), while Johnny Gavin remains the top-scoring Norwich City player to date. During his career between 1948 and 1955 he scored a total of 122 goals.

The record home attendance for a Norwich City match is 43,984 for the sixth round FA Cup match against Leicester City held on 30 March 1963.

The highest transfer fee received for a Norwich player to date is the £7.25 million paid by West Ham United for Dean Ashton in January 2006.

The most spent by the club on a player to date was the £3.5 million for Robert Earnshaw from West Bromwich Albion in January 2006.

TEN FACTS ABOUT NORWICH SPEEDWAY

The Firs Stadium on Aylsham Road, the home of speedway in Norwich, held its first race meeting on Sunday 17 August 1930.

The Firs began as a grass track but was soon converted and the first proper dirt track meeting held there was on 13 September 1931 between Norwich and Staines. The match was won by Norwich 33–21.

The first time racing was held under an ACU permit was on 25 June 1933 with Australia v the Rest.

In 1938 the Firs was considered the fastest track in the country.

In the years immediately after the Second World War the gate numbers showed an average attendance of 20,000. In 1947 alone, 460,000 passed through the turnstiles.

Norwich Stars carried off their first senior title when they secured the National Trophy in 1955.

The Stars were invited into the National League Division One in 1952 and finished runners-up in the league in 1958 and 1963.

In 1958 Norwich Stars rider Ove Fundin was recognised to be the best rider in the world. He won the World Championship on a total of four occasions.

Norwich Speedway was brought to an abrupt end. The last ever race meeting was held on 31 October 1963 and the Firs site sold for redevelopment to a property company on 3 March 1964.

The last announcer at the stadium was Bill Smith, known as the 'Voice of the Firs'. He was also the last chairman of the Norwich Speedway Supporters' Club.

THE STARS OF NORWICH SPEEDWAY

Ove Fundin
Bert Spencer
Raymond 'Billy' Bales
Phil Clarke
Titch Read
Wilf Jay
Cyril Roger
Derek Strutt
Dick Wise

Johnny Chamberlain
Wal Morton
Ted Bravery
Geoff Pymar
Aub Lawson
Paddy Mills
Bert Spencer
Reg Trott

BOXIANA

Henry Skipper was a notable boxer in the late eighteenth century who fought against the notable pugilists of the day such as Algar and Henry. He spent his later years as a dyer in Norwich and died there on 21 February 1802.

Mr Grint, a dyer, and Mr Purdy, a weaver, 'neither of whom had any pretentions to pugilistic science', fought for an hour near Bishop Bridge in Norwich in 1822. Purdy became insensible and died three days later. Grint was tried and found guilty for the crime at the Assizes and received three months' imprisonment.

In June 1823 a prize fight took place near Wymondham for £5 a side between Mr Gales and Mr Dann. After a hard milling for over an hour, during which seventy rounds were fought 'without the least display of skill or science', Mr Dann was obliged to give in.

In July 1827 a well contested prize fight took place at Bessingham between Rix and Sharpens for £5 a side. The former beat his opponent, after fighting seventy-eight rounds in 45 minutes.

At a prize fight on Costessey Common in February 1839 between Mr Rix and Mr Clarke, sixty-three rounds were fought in 1 hour and 20 minutes. Rix was the victor but it was recorded 'Never were two men more severely punished by one another.'

Jem Mace, the 'father' of modern scientific boxing, was born at Beeston-next-Mileham in 1831. Known as 'The Swaffham Gypsy' he began as a bare-knuckle boxer and won the title of Champion of England in June 1861. Mace went to America in 1868 and toured with the celebrated American boxer John C. Heenan, giving exhibitions of boxing with gloves on. In 1870 Jem defeated Tom Allen at Kenner, near New Orleans, Louisiana. He successfully defended his title twice more. After a brief return to England, Mace was back in America in 1876 for a historic early clash under Queensberry Rules, where he defeated Bill Davis at Virginia City, Nevada. From 1877 to 1882 Mace toured Australia and New Zealand where his boxing exhibitions paved the way for the worldwide acceptance of gloved boxing. Mace died in Jarrow, Durham, in 1910. He was inducted into the Ring Boxing Hall of Fame in 1954 and the International Boxing Hall of Fame in 1990.

Local boxing legend Arthur 'Ginger' Sadd of Norwich boxed from 1929 to 1951. He was a top ten middleweight contender, a world-class fighter, he fought over 200 bouts and held both the Eastern Area Welterweight and Middleweight titles. He beat many of the top welter- and middleweight contenders of his era, yet only got one shot at a British title when he challenged the redoubtable Jock McAvoy for the British and Empire middleweight titles in May 1939. Sadd was not a big puncher, but a master craftsman in the ring. He continued to box when he was well past his prime but his boxing skills were enough for him to hold his own with the best middleweights of the 1940s. A great local character to the end, 'Ginger' sadly passed away on 10 April 1992.

LEATHER ON WILLOW

Salix alba Caerulea, or the Cricket Bat Willow, is a more upright genus of the white willow tree. It was found in Norfolk in about the year 1700 and was declared to be the supreme wood for a cricket bat. Cuttings from this original tree have been propagated ever since.

A two-day cricket match commenced on the Lakenham Ground, Norwich, on 23 July 1868 between the Carrow Club and a team of 'Aboriginal Australians'. The newspaper commented 'the Australians showed surprising skill with the bat.' In the first day's play they made 177 against the measly Carrow score of 82.

In May 1823 a cricket match was played at Hockwold-cum-Wilton between eleven married and eleven single women for eleven pairs of gloves. The married women won.

A cricket match at Litcham in June 1825 was played between six members of the Alexander family of Hingham and the five Cushions of Shipdham against the village of Litcham for stakes of 22 sovereigns a-side. The match was won by the 'families' by one wicket: Families 55-88; Litcham 82-60.

The Last Ball of the Season.

During the severe snows and icy snap of February 1827 a cricket match was played on the ice of Diss Mere. Commencing at 10.00 a.m. it was contested until dusk in the presence of about 1,500 spectators. A similar match took place on the frozen Scoulton Mere in December 1840 between two selected XIs from Hingham.

BILLY BLUELIGHT

Norwich character 'Billy Bluelight,' real name William Cullum, was born on one of the hard-up streets of the city in about 1860. He received no formal education but taught himself to read and worked for a number of years at Caley's chocolate factory. He was never known for his academic prowess but my word could he run! Billy would race against the river boats, such as the SS *Jenny Lind*, from Foundry Bridge in Norwich to Great Yarmouth and then back again with the boat's return journey where he would hold his running cap out at the end of the gang plank for people to show their appreciation with a small donation. Now, some say he had a bicycle or two stashed along the route but the passengers certainly saw him running along the river bank for long sections of the journey. Either way, with his merry rhyme, 'My name is Billy Bluelight, my age is forty-five, I hope to get to Carrow bridge before the boat arrive,' Billy certainly made the journey under his own steam for many a year and indeed for years after he was forty-five. Billy passed away in 1949 but remains a fondly remembered Norwich character. There is even a sculpture of him at Wherryman's Way, Bramerton.

BIG SHOTS

At Holkham, between 31 October and 17 November 1808, Mr Coke and seven other guns killed 1,131 hares, 214 pheasants, 366 partridges, 983 rabbits, 30 woodcock, 12 wood pigeons and 5 snipe.

William Bell of Norwich, a member of a shooting party at Sprowston in November 1818, killed five-and-a-half brace of golden plover with one shot – a shot said 'not to be paralleled in the annals of sporting notoriety.'

In August 1888 Lord Walsingham killed 1,058 grouse on his small moor at Blubberhouses in Yorkshire.

A male sea eagle with a wingspan of 7ft 3in was shot at Hunstanton Hall in December 1835.

In little more than three days in January 1839, Sir Richard Sutton and a small party of friends shot 1,313 pheasants and an immense quantity of rabbits, hares, partridges and woodcock on his estate at Lynford and Tofts.

IS THAT A BOWLER OR A COKE, SIR?

Edward Coke of Holkham Hall requested a special hat from James Locke, hat maker of St James's, London, in 1849. It was to be a close-fitting, low-crowned hat to protect his gamekeepers from low-hanging branches when out riding and perhaps even a blow from a poacher when going about their duties. This special order hat was known as the 'Coke'. The design proved to be extremely popular and at one time was *de rigueur* for all London businessmen . . . except it became known by the name of the company that went on to mass-manufacture them – Bowler Brothers.

SPORTS ROUNDUP

One of the only surviving Camping Lands once used for the play of the violent game Camp Ball is in Swaffham.

The oldest surviving amateur football club in Norfolk is North Walsham Town FC, formed in 1879.

The Norwich race meeting of June 1838 on Mousehold Heath was attended by 30,000 spectators.

The Revd Arthur Wilson Upcher, Rector of Ashwellthorpe and Wreningham for forty-eight years, rowed number seven in the Cambridge boat for the second ever university boat race and the first to be contested from Westminster to Putney in 1836.

The first recorded angling match in the county took place on 18 August 1859 at Limpenhoe Reach on the Yare, for prizes given by Mr C.J. Greene of Rose Lane, Norwich. The total weight of fish taken by the twenty-eight competitors in the course of 8 hours was 16 stones 7lb 1oz. Mr G. Harman secured first prize with a catch of 33lb 3oz.

Motor racing legend 'Tim' Birkin (1896–1933), will forever be one of the 'Bentley Boys', who cut quite a dash with his white helmet and blue polka dot scarf whipping out behind him as he sped around the Grand Prix tracks of Britain and Europe in the 1920s. At one time he held the outright lap record at Brooklands at 137.96mph. Birkin had a number of Norfolk connections: he owned Tacolneston Hall and lived at Shadwell Court near Thetford but above all he loved Blakeney and lies in the cemetery there.

FOOD & DRINK

An old saying, that was quite true, stated Norwich had a church for every month and a pub for every day of the year. Incidentally, the oldest surviving pub in Norwich is the Adam and Eve in Bishopgate, built in 1249 as a brewhouse for the workers building the cathedral.

In 1810 it was recorded that William Durrant, a gardener living in Oxburgh, made it his habit to eat 1,095 red herrings, chew 18lb of tobacco and take 365oz of snuff every year. These pleasures annually cost him the then grand sum of £13 18s 10d.

Christmas Fare: Over three days in December 1810 it took twelve carriages, each one pulled by six horses and having ten stages (and using 720 horses) to draw the 800 hampers of poultry, sausages and game from Norwich to London.

At the sale of effects of Gunton Hall in 1839 the prices for some of the wines, liquors and beer included: Griffith's port (1830) sold at 81s per dozen; Fontignac at £8 per dozen; curaçao £13 per dozen, brandy £9 per dozen and ale at £4 a barrel.

9

TRANSPORT

FIRSTS & ONLYS

The first Turnpike Road Act in Norfolk was granted in 1695 for the improvement of the main road between Wymondham and Attleborough.

The first Norwich, Aylsham and Cromer coach commenced running on 23 April 1810. It ran from no. 21 Lobster Lane in Norwich to the Red Lion Inn, Cromer, on Mondays, Wednesdays and Fridays and returned on Tuesdays, Thursdays and Saturdays. The proprietor of the service was Mr W. Spanton.

An exhibition of the earliest form of bicycles, known as the Pedestrian Hobby-Horse, was made in Norwich in April 1819.

The first steam-driven coach in Norfolk was trialled at Witton near Norwich before a large crowd in May 1843. Despite the steam being turned on, the coach did not move. When pushed, it started

a short distance, then stopped. Eventually lifted from the road 'the wheels went round with alarming velocity' but failed to impress the observers.

The first screw steamboat to be built in Norwich was launched from Field's boatbuilding yard, Carrow Abbey, on 10 March 1868. Named the *Alexandra* and owned by John Hart Boughen, she was intended for passenger transport on local rivers.

In 1823 a perpetual motion machine, claimed to have been working continually since its invention seven years earlier, was exhibited at Mr Chestnut's at St Giles, Norwich. Local authorities were tipped off and discovered the machine was a fraud and dismissed it from the city.

The first railway in Norfolk opened on 30 April 1844. Spanning 20 miles it connected Norwich and Great Yarmouth.

The fastest run on the Great Eastern Railway was accomplished by a special train, the *Prince of Wales*. It travelled from St Pancras to King's Lynn, a distance of 98 miles, in 1 hour and 55 minutes.

The first recorded deployment of a parachute over Norfolk was in September 1839 when a monkey was dropped by parachute onto Mousehold Heath during a balloon ascent.

The first person to fly over Norwich in an aircraft was Bentfield C. Hucks on 10 August 1912.

ROAD RAGE

Boy racers are nothing new. Witnesses were called for by Norwich authorities after reports were received of 'reprehensible conduct' whereby the Day and Times stagecoaches raced on the road from London to Norwich, covering 112 miles in less than 11 hours.

In the early nineteenth century Adam Burrell, the carrier between Flitcham and Lynn, was notorious for taking between 6 and 7 hours to drive the 10 miles between the two, hence his nickname, 'Adam Slow.'

In April 1823 a Norwich sand seller drove his cart and pair of horses up the flight of ten steps from Davey Place to the Castle ditches. The horses did this with much ease and without injury – much to the astonishment of spectators.

LAST TRAIN DEPARTED

Fifteen redundant or lost railway stations of Norfolk:
Bluestone (situated between Aylsham and Corpusty, Midland & Great Northern, closed 1916)
Catfield (Midland & Great Northern, closed 1959)
Cromer High (Great Eastern Railway, closed 1960)
Docking (Great Eastern Railway, closed 1952)
Felmingham (Midland & Great Northern, closed 1959)
Guestwick (Midland & Great Northern, closed 1959)
Holkham (Midland & Great Northern, closed 1952)
Honing (Midland & Great Northern 1882–1959)
Potter Heigham (Midland & Great Northern, closed 1959)
Melton Constable (Midland & Great Northern, closed 1964)
Mundesley (Norfolk and Suffolk Joint Railway, closed 1964)
North Walsham Town (Midland & Great Northern, closed 1966)
Trimingham (Norfolk and Suffolk Joint Railway, closed 1953)
Wells-next-the-Sea (Great Eastern Railway, closed 1964)
Yarmouth Beach (Midland & Great Northern, closed 1959)

A STATION IN A CLASS OF ITS OWN

Gunton station in Thorpe Market was built by Lord Suffield primarily for his own convenience. His desire was to bring the railway to North Norfolk, or rather, as some would suggest, he wanted to view his estate from a railway. Suffield became a major investor in the original East Norfolk Railway Company which built the railway from Norwich to Cromer. Gunton station, complete with his lordship's own personal waiting room, opened on 29 July 1876. Although the station building is closed to the public and has become a private residence, the line remains active and the lovingly restored station may be seen when the trains stop on the opposite platform.

LINES

WRITTEN

ON THE LATE FATAL ACCIDENT,

Which occurred on the Hunstanton Railway, near Lynn,

AUGUST 3rd, 1863.

Luke 13 ch. 4 & 5 v.

Arise my Muse, put on thy garb
  Of mourning for the dead ;
Let every mind with awe be fill'd,
  And serious thoughts be led.

For mortal death is solemn—grave,
  Come how and when it will ;
But when 'tis sudden and severe,
  More melancholy still.

'Twas on the third of August, when
  We left our friends at home,
To seek the cliffs at Hunstanton,
  And on the shore to roam.

The train was fill'd from end to end,
  (One Shilling was the fare,)
For hundreds came, both old and young,
  From distance far and near.

Now all were gay and merry too ;
  The hours soon pass'd away ;
We sail'd and row'd, we bath'd and splash'd,
  We had a pleasant day.

The crowds were great, and eager too,
  As night shades drew apace ;
" Divide the train " the master calls,
  So each one took their place.

The monster whistled,— on they start,
  The first part steam'd away ;
The second engine ready stands
  The starting bell t' obey.

Then on we sped with merry glee,
  To seek our own dear home ;
When, Lo ! a Beast our way besets,
  Which cast a sudden gloom.

Then shrieks and cries the air did fill,
  And all was fear and dread ;
As wreck and ruin all around,
  Were strew'd upon the dead.

Five mangled bodies in their gore,
  Were stretched upon the ground ;
And many more with broken limbs
  Distress'd—they lay around.

There's builder LAIRD (with wife since dead,)
  CLARKE, PALMER, BROWN and CLARK ;
With *Batterham, Bartle, Jickling* too,
  All bleeding in the dark.

The news soon spread throughout the town,
  Physicians soon were there ;
And quick a good Samaritan
  Did oil and wine prepare.

There's CAPTAIN DENNES, carried home,
  When woe ! his friends betide.—
He made his will, then lingered on
  Till morning light,—and died.

And now dear friends, of old King's Lynn,
  Come sympathize with sorrow ;
In health and joy we spend to-day,
  We are dead and gone to-morrow.

So now prepare to meet the foe,
  While gathered round the grave ;
Repent and to your Saviour turn,
  Whilst health and time you have.

For Oh ! a gracious Saviour, He
  With out-stretched arms, now stands,
Repent—Believe—be Saved, He cries ;—
  Behold my side !—my hands !

ONE PENNY EACH.

The profits to be given in aid of the Funds of the West Norfolk and Lynn Hospital.

Printed and Sold by J. M. Matsell, 10, High Street, Lynn.

10

DEATH & RELIGION

ABOUT THE CHURCHES

The origins of the Diocese of Norwich can be traced back to the seventh century when St Felix first fixed his see at Dunwich and then moved to Elmham in 673. It was thence moved to Thetford in 1070 and finally to Norwich ahead of the new cathedral building in 1094.

Norwich Cathedral's original spire was constructed in wood and was burned down by townsmen during rioting in 1272. Rebuilt, again in wood, it was blown down in the great hurricane of 1362. A third wooden spire was struck by lightning in 1463. The stone spire we know today dates from 1480.

The church of St Peter and St Paul, Knapton, has one of the most remarkable double hammer-beam roofs in the country. Constructed in 1503 it is one of the widest known, crossing about 12 metres in a single span – a truly remarkable feat. A host of angels gaze down upon the viewer giving the whole vision a heaven-like quality.

A unique feature of St Nicholas Church, North Walsham, is its Royal Arms Board; one side bears the arms of Cromwell's Commonwealth, while the other features the arms of Charles II.

Four or five churches have stood on the site of St Nicholas' Church, Dilham. The first recorded church (though it is thought there was an earlier religious building there) was built by William de Glanville in about 1125. The second, larger edifice with a tower was built by Sir Roger Gyney in about 1370. After falling into disrepair, this church was demolished in 1835 and another was built shortly afterwards. In turn this was found unsound, and the church seen today was built by Cornish & Gaymer in 1931.

The bells of St Nicholas' Church, North Walsham, were rung all day for the town's Ascensiontide Fayre on 15 May 1724. Between 9.00 and 10.00 a.m. the following morning, the tower collapsed. The only person injured was the local doctor who was walking through the churchyard at the time and he suffered a cut to his ankle from a flying flint. A second fall occurred on 17 February 1836 when heavy wintry gales brought down the north segment of the tower, sending earthquake-like tremors through the town and leaving the bells in a mass of ruins. The remaining east wall of the belfry stage was then dismantled as a safety precaution.

John Hall and William Palmer were brought before Norfolk Assizes on 9 April 1839 and found guilty of stealing one of the bells from the collapsed tower of North Walsham church. Accomplice John Daniels turned Queen's evidence and stated they had taken the bell away in a cart, broken it up and attempted to sell the metal for scrap in Norwich. Found guilty of the crime, each of the accused received one year's imprisonment.

5,040 changes of Plain Bob Triples were rung for the first time, in 3 hours and 17 minutes at the Church of St Peter Mancroft, Norwich, in 1715.

At 23,000sq ft, the Church of St Nicholas in Great Yarmouth is the largest parish church in England by floor surface area.

St Helen's Church at Ranworth is known as the 'Cathedral of the Broads'.

St Michael the Archangel Church at Booton is known as the 'Cathedral of the Fields'.

The churchyard of St George's in Tombland in Norwich is estimated to hold up to 10,000 burials.

The Roman Catholic Cathedral Church of St John the Baptist in Norwich was only consecrated as a cathedral church in 1976. Built on the site of the Norwich City Gaol between 1882 and 1910 to designs by George Gilbert Scott Jr, it was originally opened as the Church of John the Baptist on 8 December 1910.

The font canopy in the church of St Botolph at Trunch dates from about 1500. Ornately carved in oak with slender pillars forming a hexagonal enclosure it is one of only four of its kind in England The others are to be found in St Mary's, Luton (1350), St Peter Mancroft, Norwich (1450) and Durham Cathedral (1680).

Carved on the fifteenth-century font within St Giles' Church, Colby, is a depiction of the Madonna and Child in the Seat of Wisdom. This is a rare survival indeed as most of these depictions were commonly destroyed by the hammers of Anglican or Puritan iconoclasts.

St Nicholas' Chapel, King's Lynn, is the largest chapel in England. The building dates almost entirely from the fifteenth century, though the tower is earlier and the spire was added by Sir George Gilbert Scott in 1869.

In November 1816, Buckoo, a Bengali man and native of Calcutta, was publicly baptised at Burnham Market Church with the name of John Henry Martin by the Revd John Glasse.

On 3 August 1879 Wells church tower was struck by lightning and the ensuing fire burned the entire church out, even destroying the fine peal of bells. Rebuilt at a cost of £10,000 the church was reopened on 18 April 1883.

Preacher Thomas Olivers (1725–99) made an unsuccessful attempt to introduce Methodism into Yarmouth in 1754. Coming to the town on a Sunday, Olivers and a friend attempted to preach in the open air but were mercilessly assailed with dirt, stones and missiles of every description and driven out of the town.

DYING OFF

When she died aged 105 in February 1803, Mary Helson of East Ruston had lived in three centuries and left behind her a progeny of eighty children, great-grandchildren and great-great-grandchildren.

In November 1880 the body of Henry Jonathan Minns, lay clerk at Norwich Cathedral and a well-known local tenor, was discovered suspended by the neck upon a ladder in the presbytery triforium over St Luke's Chapel at the cathedral. The inquest returned a verdict of suicide while of unsound mind.

Sarah Pickwood of St Mary's, Norwich, died in December 1806 aged forty-nine. She was recorded as 'one of the most enormous cases of dropsy on record.' To ease her suffering, in the course of 50 months she was tapped 38 times and discharged 350 gallons of fluid.

The Revd John Cross Morphew, the once 'respectably connected' rector of Cley and Walpole St Peter, died after cutting his own throat with a razor in the Fleet Prison for debtors in London in April 1824.

In October 1813 Mr J. Youngs (aged eighty-five) of St Peter Hungate, Norwich, was carried in his sedan chair to vote at the mayor's election. On his return home he immediately expired.

When James Church died in 1814 he had been sexton of St Peter Parmountergate Church, Norwich, for fifty years, and had buried about 3,000 people.

Robert King, formerly servant to William Paston, 2nd Earl of Yarmouth, was buried at Skeyton in May 1727 after his death in the 103rd year of his life. Curiously, it is recorded that he had grown an entire set of new teeth about ten years before his death.

When Swaffham gardener Thomas Chesney died aged eighty-eight in 1815 he had never travelled further than 4 miles from his home.

When William Coward died in July 1822 aged eighty-five after serving fifty-four years as parish clerk at St Margaret's, Lynn, he was borne to his grave by six gravediggers and the pall was supported by six parish clerks.

PREPARED TO MEET THEIR DOOM

Norwich worsted weaver John Minns anticipated his death and bought his coffin and used it as a cupboard for sixteen years before he died aged ninety-four in 1815.

When Benjamin Smith died at Lynn aged ninety-three in 1829, his gravestone had stood in St Margaret's churchyard for nearly ten years with blanks left to be filled in for the day and date of his death.

When Ursula Hewytt of Breckles died, her will of 1674 (proved in 1678) stated she was to be buried in an upright position. Her black ledger slab in the chancel bears the inscription 'STAT UT VIXIT ERECTA', meaning 'as upright in death as she was in life'.

In 2011 Downham Market pensioner Joy Tomkins had the message 'Do Not Resuscitate' tattooed across her chest – just in case she was involved in an accident or fell ill and attempts were made to revive her. Furthermore, to avoid any confusion she also had P.T.O. and an arrow tattooed on her back.

WHAT A WAY TO GO!

On 18 February 1832 Thomas Foyson (aged fifty-three), proprietor of the Calvert Street Vinegar Works in Norwich, fell into a vat of vinegar he was gauging and drowned.

Mr Walter Morgan of Morgan's Brewery on King Street, Norwich, met his death by falling into a vat of beer in May 1845.

James Bullard (aged sixty-six), many years master of the Bethel Hospital for Lunatics in Norwich, died on 25 April 1813 from a wound to his stomach inflicted by a patient engaged in mowing the hospital lawn.

When the Norwich and Newmarket Mail coach overturned in a deep drain while proceeding through Methwold in February 1833, Mr Booty the coachman was fallen on by one of the horses and suffocated.

In February 1806 James Coleman was tolling the bell in the parish church at Swardeston when the crown and cannons broke from the bell, sending it crashing to the floor and killing him on the spot.

During a violent gale in January 1808, Mr and Mrs Graham were killed when their chimney collapsed in on the roof of their house on Cockey Lane (now London Street), Norwich.

During the Napoleonic Wars the detached tower of East Dereham church was used as a lock-up for French prisoners of war en route to the prison at Norman Cross. One such prisoner was Lieutenant Jean de Narde (aged twenty-eight) the son of a notary public of St Mâlo, who contrived to escape and made off on 6 October 1799. He took refuge in a tree on the Scarning Road and when ordered to come down, he refused, and thus was shot down 'like a crow'.

In August 1848 Thomas Ireson (aged ten) thought it would be good idea to tie himself to the tail of a cow at Mattishall. The infuriated animal kicked him to death.

Joseph Penny of Yarmouth tempted fate by playing Neptune at the Peace Festival in 1814 and drowned while boating three years later.

The Revd Robert Forby, Rector of Fincham and author of *The Vocabulary of East Anglia*, was found drowned in his bath in December 1825.

At a convivial night at the Three Turks at Charing Cross, Norwich, in October 1835, local artisan William Cork was singing the song composed upon the death of General Wolfe and after repeating the words 'And I to death must yield', instantly fell down and died.

After performing the death scene from *Othello* (complete with dramatic fall to the ground), to an audience at the Swan Inn at Downham in November 1842, John Vare returned home and died.

On 26 May 1863 vocalists Charles Marsh and Henry Wharton attempted to ascend the Nelson Monument at Great Yarmouth, Marsh performing 'God Save the Queen' on his violin as he went with Wharton accompanying on the banjo. Both arrived at the summit but Marsh went on to scale the figure of Britannia. Achieving this feat, he stood atop the figure and waved to the crowd beneath, but while descending lost his grasp of Britannia's trident handle, slipped, fell from the plinth, rebounded into space and fell with his arm outstretched to the base of the column – some 114ft. His death was recorded as 'instantaneous'.

Norfolk and Kent cricketer William Pilch died of 'mortification of the big toe' on 4 September 1866.

Three sisters, Clara, Eleanor and Ida Vipan, were drowned while wandering upon the treacherous sands at Holkham on 9 July 1896.

WHAT A SEND OFF!

The most significant funeral performed at Bromholm Priory was that of Sir John Paston who was brought from London to the priory for internment. In the roll of expenses for this grand event was a note that one man was engaged for three continuous days to flay the beasts for the feast viz; 41 pigs, 49 calves and 10 oxen. With the meat were 1,300 eggs, 20 gallons of milk, and 8 of cream. In addition 15 combs of malt were brewed for the occasion, 13 barrels of beer were provided, 27 of ale and a 'runlet of red wine of 15 gallons'. There was even a barber occupied for five days beforehand, presumably smartening up the monks for the ceremony. The funeral cortège of carriages, carts and entourage was said to have been so long its tail was still been passing through the town of North Walsham (about 4 miles away) when the front wagons entered the priory gates. The 'reke of the torches at the dirge' was so intense, a glazier was brought in to remove two window panes to allow the fumes to escape.

REST IN PEACE?

Sir Thomas Browne, the notable Norwich physician and philosopher, was not allowed to rest in peace after his death in October 1682. His grave was discovered while preparing another in the sanctuary of St Peter Mancroft Church in Norwich in 1840. After a brief examination, most of his bones were reburied, with the exception of his skull, hair and coffin plate, which were removed by local chemist Robert Fitch. Later presented by a Dr Lubbock to the Norfolk and Norwich Hospital, it was displayed in their museum for many years afterwards until 1922 when eventually, after an undignified squabble about its cost and value, the skull was finally reinterred in a specially made casket with full burial rites that referred to it being 317 years old!

SAINTS & RELICS

The river channel at Castle Rising is said to have been navigated by St Felix of Burgundy as far as Babbingly when he landed there in AD 630 and the first Christian chapel in Norfolk was erected near the site. The present church that stands there in tragic ruin was built to replace the earlier structure in the fourteenth century.

East Dereham contains the site of a monastery founded by St Withburga in the seventh century. A holy well at the western end of St Nicholas' Church supposedly began to flow when her body was stolen by monks from Ely in AD 974.

St Wolfeius is mentioned in the writings of William Worcester who recorded him as the first hermit of St Benet Hulme. Wolfeius died during the eleventh century, on 9 December which thus became his feast day.

St Walstan was born either in Bawburgh in Norfolk or Blytheburgh in Suffolk. When he was only twelve, he left his parents' home and travelled to Taverham where he worked as a farm labourer.

He dedicated his life to farming and the care of farm animals and remains the patron saint of farms, farmers, farmhands, ranchers and husbandrymen. After a vision from an angel, Walstan died while at work scything a hay crop on 30 May 1016. His body was laid on a cart, pulled by two white oxen. At three points along the journey the oxen stopped and a spring arose, and the cortège ended up at Bawburgh, where he was buried.

St Edmund landed at Hunstanton in 855 to be crowned King of East Anglia. St Edmund's Chapel on the cliffs at St Edmund's Point, Hunstanton, now in ruins, was erected in memory of this event in 1272.

St William of Norwich was a popular rather than a formal papal canonisation. The boy was claimed to have been martyred by Jews in mockery of Christ's crucifixion on Mousehold Heath in 1144. His bones were retained in a shrine at Norwich Cathedral. Thomas of Monmouth, a Norwich Benedictine monk, recorded the incident and wonders performed by the remains in *The Life and Miracles of St. William of Norwich* (1173).

The Shrine of Our Lady at Walsingham was a major pilgrimage site of national importance in medieval Britain; many miracles were sought and claimed at the shrine where one of their most prized relics was a phial of the Virgin's milk. Several English kings visited the shrine, including Henry III, Edward I, Edward III, Henry VI, Henry VII and Henry VIII.

The head of John the Baptist was claimed to be at Trimingham. It was, in fact, a life-size alabaster head of the saint that was kept at the church and pilgrims in this country came to the church to the shrine altar, rather than make the journey to Amiens Cathedral where a relic said to be the real head of John the Baptist was kept.

The dado screen at St Mary's Church, Worstead, includes a rare depiction of Christian martyr Wilgefortis, otherwise known as Uncumber, with her facial hair. Her father wanted her to marry the King of Sicily, but she had taken a vow of virginity. So she prayed to become unattractive: the result was that a moustache and beard grew on her face and her suitor withdrew. Her father subsequently had her crucified. While on the cross she prayed that all who remembered her passion should be liberated from all encumbrances and troubles.

The Good Sword of Winfarthing was preserved in the church of St Mary the Virgin in the village for many years and drew people from some considerable distances bearing gifts and offerings to its shrine in the hope it may help them. The sword was said to have been left in the church by a thief who had claimed sanctuary there and had curiously become endowed with great power in effecting the wishes of devotees, especially in the location of missing objects and even losing unwanted husbands! Until it too was lost.

O, HOLY ROOD OF BROMHOLM

A portion of the True Cross upon which Jesus Christ had been crucified was brought to Bromholm Abbey and incorporated into its rood screen. Miracles ascribed to this relic included the cure of blindness, cure of the sick and it was claimed one pilgrim had been raised from the dead!

So famous was the 'Holy Rood' of Bromholm it entered into popular parlance as an exclamation and features in Langland's *Vision Concerning Piers Plowman*, Sir Walter Scott's *Ivanhoe* and in the Reeve's Tale in Chaucer's *Canterbury Tales*:

> The miller's fall started her out of sleep.
> 'Help!' she screamed. 'Holy Cross of Bromeholme keep
> Us! Lord! Into thy hands! To thee I call.'

The priory became a centre of national and international pilgrimage, with monarchs such as King Edward II (who visited in about 1313) and gentry paying their respect too.

The fate of the cross fragments is unclear: in 1424 it was recorded as being burned but in 1536 the Holy Relics of Bromholm were recorded as 'The Holy Cross of Bromholm', the girdle and milk of the Virgin, and pieces of the crosses of St. Peter and St. Andrew.' Some say it survived to the time of the Dissolution, when it was buried in secret a short distance from the priory and awaits discovery to this day.

11

NATURAL HISTORY

DID YOU KNOW?

The Cromer-Holt ridge, otherwise known as 'the Norfolk Heights' is the terminal moraine of a glacier.

Pingos are shallow water pools formed at the time of the last Ice Age some 9,000 years ago when buried ice boulders left behind by glaciation melted and caused the ground to slump. Examples of these can be found in the county at East Harling, East Walton and Foulden, but Thompson Common beats the lot with around 300 and remains one of the best-preserved pingo sites in Britain.

The planting of Thetford Forest began in 1922 and it is now the largest lowland forest in Britain, covering an area of 80 square miles.

The noted botanist the Revd Henry Bryant (1721–99) moved to the living of Colby after working as a minister in Norwich and Heydon. He took up the study of botany to occupy his mind after the death of his beloved wife. Also skilled in mathematics, the good reverend filled his life with these passions until he died in the village in 1799.

When a vault that had been closed for nine years was opened at St Peter Mancroft Church, Norwich, in March 1816, three bats were discovered; covered with mould and dust they were all 'in a state of complete torpidity', but one of them immediately took flight.

On 22 August 1891 the *Yarmouth Mercury* was the first paper to report the strange case of James Bartley 'The Modern Jonah'. While hunting whales in the vicinity of the Falkland Islands, Bartley was attempting to harpoon a whale but instead fell into its mouth and was swallowed. When the whale's stomach was finally opened, Bartley was found within and still alive! He did recover but his skin was affected by the gastric juices and remained wrinkled and deathly white.

In June 1826 it was recorded the lighthouse hill and adjacent heights at Cromer were 'literally covered' by ladybirds of an unusually large sort. In more modern times swarms of ladybirds have landed on Cromer and Sheringham in 1975 and 2009.

A specimen of the plant *valerian rubra*, raised from a seed found in a coffin that had been sealed since before 1300 that was discovered beneath the ruins of Wymondham priory church, was exhibited at the Norfolk and Norwich Horticultural Society in May 1836.

Lord Walsingham announced an attempt to reintroduce the Great Bustard to the Norfolk fens and made a public appeal for the protection of these birds in the press in October 1900. Sadly the reintroduction was unsuccessful.

A herring measuring 17.5in long by 7.5in in girth, and weighing 13oz, was caught near Yarmouth in 1853. In November 1870, a mackerel was caught near the town weighing 2lb 11oz. It's length was 19in and it had a girth of 10.25in.

A fine specimen of the Opah fish *(Zeus Imperialis)* measuring 3ft 3in long and 1ft 10in across was captured alive at Hunstanton in July 1839.

John Hunt, a Norwich engraver, produced *British Ornithology*, his three-volume work published in Norwich, between 1815 and 1822. It is one of the earliest and most ambitious attempts to describe and illustrate the wild bird species of the nation.

John Curtis (1791–1862), engraver, eminent naturalist and the author of the great work *British Entomology*, was a native of Norwich and learned his engraving skills while in the city in the workshop of his father, Charles Morgan Curtis.

Hundreds of birds including larks and starlings were drawn to the Happisburgh light during a storm in November 1845.

Syderstone Common is one of only two inland locations in the UK where the rare and protected natterjack toad (*Epidalea calamita*, formerly *Bufo calamita*) may still be found.

Wells-born Dr Sydney Long (1870–1939) was the founder of the Norfolk Naturalists' Trust, established in 1926. Now known as the Norfolk Wildlife Trust, they maintain sixty nature reserves covering nearly 10,000 acres of coast, broad, heath, marsh and fen in the county and has a membership of 35,000.

Thirteen of the sixteen species of bat found in the UK can be found in Norfolk.

The most impressive fossil found in the county in recent years was the West Runton Elephant, a fossilised skeleton of a Steppe Mammoth found in the cliffs of West Runton in 1990. The find is the largest nearly complete example of its species ever found in the world and is the oldest found in the United Kingdom.

NORFOLK'S UNCOMMON BUTTERFLIES

Dark Green Fritillary *(Argynnis aglaja)*
Dingy Skipper *(Erynnis tages)*
Grizzled Skipper *(Pyrgus malvae)*
Silver-studded Blue *(Plebejus argus)*
Swallowtail *(Papilio machaon)*
White-letter Hairstreak *(Strymonidia w-album)*
White Admiral *(Ladoga Camilla)*
Grayling *(Hipparchia semele)*

THE BEST & WORST OF THE WEATHER

Highest temperature 36.2°C at Hillington on 9 August 1911.
Lowest temperature -18.9°C at Santon Downham on 23 January 1963.

Sunniest year	1911, with 2,000 hours of sun recorded over the county.
Driest year	1921, when only 10.5in of rain fell at Outwell.
Wettest year	1912, with a total of 40.74in of rainfall at Norwich.
Wettest day	26 August 1912, when 7.31in of rainfall was recorded at Brundall.
Strongest wind	108mph, recorded at Cromer on 3 January 1976.
Snowiest year	1963, with sixty-four days of laying snow at Santon Downham.
White Christmases (in Norfolk)	1906, 1917, 1923, 1927, 1938, 1970, 1981.

During a thunderstorm over Norwich on 7 July 1833 a fireball about the size of a man's head fell upon the thatched roof of the Black Tower, destroying the society of artisans' observatory.

A massive hailstorm hit Norwich in 1843 causing floods and covered the streets with 5in of hailstones. This event and the suffering it caused led to the formation of the General Hailstorm Society, an insurance company that later merged with Norwich Union.

The year 1888 in Norfolk was extraordinary in meteorological annals. There had been rain akin to February through the summer months and March gales in November. There was snow during harvest and primroses blossomed in the open air on the eve of December, indeed strawberries were gathered at Swainsthorpe on Christmas morning.

FLOOD

The most significant Norfolk floods of the twentieth century:

1912: It had been a very rainy season when Norfolk was hit by a 30-hour deluge, causing rivers to rise and flood across the county, including Norwich. Some 15,000 suffered damage to their homes, 2,000 were left homeless and 4 people lost their lives.

1938: On the night of 12 February 1938 a nor'-westerly gale and high waves breached the sand hills at Horsey flooding 7,500 acres of low-lying hinterland and entered part of the Broads, killing thousands of fish.

1947: On 7 March 1947 an inch of rain fell in a few hours and could not soak into the still-icy ground. Snowmelt followed rapidly and the big rivers rose by a foot an hour. Consequently the rivers of Fenland on the Norfolk and Cambridgeshire borders swelled, flooding acres of farmland and wrecking many homes.

1953: During the night of Saturday 31 January 1953 and morning of 1 February 1953 the coast of Norfolk, along with other coastal areas of East Anglia, were hit by a wall of water during a fierce storm. Hundreds of homes were destroyed and a number of lives were lost.

12

THE COAST

A COASTAL MISCELLANY

The Norfolk coast stretches for nearly 100 miles from Hopton-on-Sea to The Wash.

Three-quarters of the North Norfolk coastline is designated an Area of Outstanding Natural Beauty.

The Wash is the largest estuarine system in the United Kingdom and contains England's largest official nature reserve, providing an internationally important habitat for fifteen species of birds. It is home to 6,000 common seals and harbours a tenth of Britain's saltmarsh.

The only east coast resort to face west is Hunstanton.

The sunset over Heacham beach can take as long as five-and-a-half hours.

The fishing and farming town of Lin, Lenne or Leuna, was known for trading and salt pans before the Norman Conquest.

In 1203 Lynn's foreign trade was such that the total duty collected was the fourth highest in any south or east coast port, including London.

The first recorded use of 'Great Yarmouth' was in 1272, during the reign of Edward I when the title was given to distinguish it from Little Yarmouth, or Southtown.

The 'Seven Burnhams by the Sea' are: Burnham Norton, Burnham Overy, Burnham Thorpe, Burnham Deepdale, Burnham Westgate, Burnham Ulph and Burnham Sutton. To remember this there is the mnemonic: Nelson Of Thorpe Died Well Under Sail.

Wells gained a dreadful reputation for wrecking ships in the thirteenth century and it stuck for centuries afterwards. 'Wells bitefingers' is the cruel name derived from the desperate stripping of dead bodies for anything of use or (especially) value washed up after shipwrecks, where the locals would literally bite or cut through the bloated fingers on the dead bodies of sailors to remove their rings.

Elizabeth Clayton of Wells worked at the local dockyard as a ship's carpenter for forty years and always dressed in men's apparel. She would drink, chew tobacco and keep company only with workmen. A robust woman, it was recalled when she died in March 1805 that 'she never permitted anyone to insult her with impunity.'

In the latter half of the nineteenth century Sheringham and Cromer had about fifty crab boats each. It was estimated that during a good season, over a million crabs would be landed at Cromer alone.

Not all were happy to 'go for a sailor' as evinced early on the morning of 11 May 1815 when a boat crew from HMS *Cadmus*, known to contain local men taken by the press gang, was attacked by a mob from both banks at the harbour mouth at Yarmouth. They faced a hail of stones and several sailors were badly wounded.

One of the 'sharpest presses' in Great Yarmouth occurred on 9 May 1805 when no fewer than 300 men were impressed; many were subsequently returned following complaint but fifty ultimately went to serve in the Royal Navy.

In St Nicholas' churchyard, Wells, lay the bodies of two veterans of the infamous mutiny on HMS *Bounty*. John Fryer (1754–1817) was the ship's Sailing Master and second-in-command to Captain Bligh. Nearby is the grave of Robert Tinkler (1770–1816) the youngest brother-in-law of Fryer and Acting Midshipman on HMS *Bounty*. Both of them were cast adrift by the mutineers in 1789, survived an epic voyage, and eventually returned to England.

AQUATICS.

Small Boy. " NOW, THEN! ALL TOGETHER ! "

In the early nineteenth century it was estimated that four-fifths of the shipwrecks in the United Kingdom were off the coasts of Norfolk and Suffolk. The series of sandbanks run from off Cromer down to Haisborough Sands and are known collectively as 'The Devil's Throat', with Winterton Ness known to mariners as 'the most fatal headland between Scotland and London'.

In one night, during the Great Gale of 1692, around 200 sail of ships and over 1,000 people were recorded as perishing in the waters off Cromer.

Daniel Defoe observed of Winterton in 1722: 'There was not a shed, nor a barn, nor a stable, nay not the pales of their fences and yards, not a hogstye but what was made of planks, beams, wales and timbers, the wreck of ships and the ruin of merchants' and mariners' fortunes.'

BESIDE THE SEASIDE

The first structure built towards realising Henry Le Strange's vision of New Hunstanton was the Golden Lion Hotel, originally named 'The New Inn'. Constructed between 1846 and 1847 the inn stood in the middle of a meadow and quite alone excepting a couple of old cottages in the vicinity. Those who did not share Le Strange's dream were soon pouring scorn on the notion and titled the inn 'Le Strange's Folly'.

Jane Austen was moved to mention Cromer as 'the best of all the sea bathing places' in *Emma*, published in 1816.

One of the most popular trips on the paddle-steamers of the Skegness Steamboat Company was the run across The Wash to Hunstanton. In 1883 the paddle-steamer *May*, one of the biggest on the east coast, was regularly steaming across The Wash filled to her capacity of 255 passengers. Leaving Skegness at 8.30 a.m., she would arrive at Hunstanton at 11.00 a.m. The return steamer journey got travellers back to Skegness for 8.00 p.m. – all for a return steamer ticket that cost 3s.

The cache of Cromer was finally sealed, in those halcyon days before the First World War, by royal patronage with a residential stay from Empress Elizabeth of Austria in 1887 and other members of German nobility throughout the 1890s.

In the late nineteenth century swimsuits were not permitted on the beaches of North Norfolk – all would have to be suitably attired from neck to knee. Anyone wishing to swim would carry their swimsuit down and get changed in a bathing machine at the water's edge. Mixed bathing was also restricted off some beaches.

On 9 August 1888 the pleasure steamer *Victoria* had set out on an unwise course from Cromer pier when her hull scraped over 'church rock' and was holed on her port side. Fortunately she did not sink and all passengers were ferried off and sent home by train. Surely this is the only instance of a ship being stranded on the top of a church!

Britain's first holiday camp was at Caister-on-Sea, opened in 1906 by John Fletcher Dodd as the Caister Socialist Holiday Camp. Campers were expected to help with chores and regulations stipulated no talking after 11.00 p.m., fines were imposed for messy tents and no alcohol was permitted.

For the 1926/7 season a weekend train ticket from London to Sheringham cost 34s 9d first class or 21s third class. A stay at Sheringham Grand cost 16s 6d per day or 115s 6d per week or at Woodford Guest House 12s 6d per day or 73s 6d per week.

RANDALL'S FOLLY

Onesiphorus Randall, born in Cley in 1798, made his fortune in speculative building construction in London. Onesiphorus enjoyed sailing and thought a house would be useful for his visits to the beach at Salthouse. He also thought it might provide a refuge for shipwrecked mariners, so he built a distinctive castellated lodge on land known as the Great Eye adjoining the beach at Salthouse. Nicknamed Randall's Folly, the building was sold to the Board of Trade after his death in 1873. After becoming a coastguard station where the rocket lifesaving apparatus was stored, and serving military purposes in two world wars, the 'folly' met its nemesis in the 1953 floods when such damage was caused to the old building by the watery incursion that it had to be pulled down.

THE LOST COAST

The Bronze Age timber circle dubbed 'Seahenge' discovered at Holme-next-the-Sea was a lost or rather a buried treasure. In 1998 fieldwork by Norfolk Archaeological Unit began on the ring that had been exposed by a sea scour. Consisting of fifty-five close-set oak timbers with a central upturned 'stump' chair or 'altar' in the centre, the timbers were removed for preservation and analysis amid much public debate. The timbers have been dated to about 2000 BC, but the reason for the construction of Seahenge, how it was built and who precisely built it will no doubt remain a subject of lively debate for years to come.

There is no mention of the town of Cromer in the Domesday survey of 1086. Instead, there was Shipden, a town that was eroded away by the indefatigable lap of the sea and what ruins remain of it lie beneath the waves.

Stretching the boundaries of Poppyland to Mundesley, a new holiday resort town was planned there; it was to be called 'Cliftonville'. Plots of land were put up for sale in 1890 and two new hotels were built and a railway link soon followed, but the dream of Cliftonville was never realised.

The rate of sea erosion at Happisburgh was well evinced by the sale deeds for what became Lighthouse Farm; when it was offered for sale in 1790 it comprised 280 acres, but when it was sold in 1852 it had depleted to just 176 acres.

Eccles suffered erosion by the sea for centuries but the final straw for the town came in the teeth of the violent storm of 4 January 1604 when the sea defences were breached and 2,000 acres of marsh, wood and arable land were inundated by seawater. Sixty-six houses and most of their occupants were swept away and smashed the main body of the parish church, leaving the disembodied tower standing over the scene of devastation like a silent sentinel.

The tower of Eccles church ended up on the beach and was a landmark observed by passing sea traffic, especially the day-trippers on the paddle-steamers, but the tower finally succumbed to the waves and fell during a storm between the hours of 6.00 and 7.00 p.m. on 23 January 1895.

THAR SHE BLOWS!

In 1588 the accounts of Nathaniel Bacon recorded the payments to over fifty men for the processing of a great whale cast up on Holkham beach in November of that year. A small selection of supplies for the work included: 'a kettell and a lantern from Mr Howsgo; six staves,

WHALE STRANDED AT WINTERTON.

a plowbeame, two leavers, a wimble, a kill heare and a block from Peter Palmer of Gounthorp; a greate pott, a latchpaine, three spites, two yron ladelles and two fleshookes, sixteen barrels from James Mytterson of Congham, eleven barrels from William Frarye; two pipes and a tonner from Robert Shyne and a lantern and skomer from Henry Page.'

In December 1626 a whale was cast on the shore at Holm by a strong nor'-westerly. It measured 57ft long and had a breadth from nose end to eye of 15½ft, 'the eyes about the same bigness as those of an ox.' In the mouth were counted forty-six teeth like the tusks of an elephant. The account concludes 'it was a male, had a pizzle about 6ft long and about a foot diameter near its body. The profit made of the whole fish was £217 6s 7d and the charge in cutting it up and managing it came to £100 or more.'

When the whaler *Enterprise* arrived at South Lynn from Greenland under the command of Captain Sanderson in August 1818 eleven 'fish' were on board. It was estimated they would produce an estimated 160 tons of oil worth about £6,000, exclusive of whalebone and by-products.

In August 1854 a whale 'of the beak species' some 29ft in length and with a girth of 21ft was washed up upon Snettisham beach. The record of this 'landing' concluded, 'When boiled, although the operation was unskilful, it produced 120 gallons of oil.'

A 48ft whale weighing about 25 tons was beached at Winterton on 5 January 1857. The body was boiled for blubber and the skin, head and tail were removed for exhibition.

Congham Oil Mill on the River Cong was built for the processing of whales transported there by horse and wagon from King's Lynn docks and the mill would produce oil from whale blubber. The whale bones were a by-product that would, in turn, be taken by road to Narborough Bone Mill where they were ground into fertiliser.

The last whale was landed at King's Lynn in 1812.

HERRING HEYDAYS

Herring has been known as a staple food source since 3000 BC.

Herring could be preserved or 'cured' by a simple process of gutting and salting. These fish could be transported over considerable distances and became an important commodity and delicacy across medieval Europe.

Archaeological digs in Great Yarmouth have revealed large quantities of fishhooks and bones on some of the lowest strata that also demonstrate human occupation. The bones are particularly from cod and herring, proving beyond a doubt the town was literally built on fishing.

In the early twentieth century as many as 30,000 vessels were involved in herring fishing off the east coast.

Through the seasons the fishing boats and industry workers followed the shoals of millions of herring down the coast of Britain. The shoals of herring, known affectionately as 'silver darlings' were caught off the north coast of Scotland and the Shetlands in the summer and then, as they migrated south, they made rich pickings all along the east coast, notably off the East Anglian coast in the autumn as they made their way to their spawning grounds in the Dover Straits and off Brittany.

ALPHABETICAL RHYME

Of useful and amusing Hints to Fishermen and their Friends,

By WILLIAM HOYLE, Gorleston.

A stands for Anchor the Fisherman's hope,
Its a very good thing, with a strong chain or rope
To ride out the Storm or keep time with the tide,
In his beautiful Smack that he watches with pride.

B will spell Binacle, close to his hand
When steering his craft away from the land,
To the grounds which he knows are oft covered with fish,
That gets him a living and make some people rich.

C stand for Capstan, the crew at it work,
And woe be the lad who his duty would shirk,
For the Skipper is blunt and would think it no sin,
To give him the sack without any tin.

D will spell Darknes through which he must go,
On cold winter nights, in frost, wind or snow
When danger is rife and fill landsmen with dread,
Even when they are snug in a warm coozey bed.

E is to Eke out the Bread, Beef and Tea,
Waste not is the motto when sailing at sea;
And when they are hundreds of miles from the shore,
It is hard to replenish an impoverished store.

F stands for Fish, a most cheering sight,
Let them be caught in the day or the night;
And if they be took with a net or a line,
God bless their toil, send them plenty of Prime.

G goes for Gaff attached to the sail
To hold it out smart, in calm or in gale,
Then up with the Peak to keep her a luff,
To steer a Smack well you must not be a muff.

H will spell Hatchway that leads to the hold,
Where they keep tackle, and water and coal,
And ballast to make her stand up with the breeze,
And carry her safe over gigantic seas.

I is for Ice, a most useful thing,
It enables the Fisher his cargo to bring
Full many a league from his dear native home,
Where fickle fortune compels him to roam.

J stands for Jack, oft a Fisherman's name,
They christened him John but that was to tame,
He spends his good money quite free on the shore,
Then to see he will go and try to earn more.

K will spell Keel of timber so strong,
It stretches from stem to stern post along,
By the rights of the law your ship to keep sound,
She never should touch on any hard ground.

L will spell Lamps with red and green glass,
To prevent sad collisions when vessels shall pass;
So keep them well trimmed to make them burn bright,
And your shipmates will sleep all the safer at night.

M stands for Moon, its the Fisherman's joy,
He's as pleased with its light as a child with a toy
For it lightens his path and makes the fish sport,
And gladdens his heart as to market they're brought.

N goes for North, on the compass card round,
If you raise it up, beneath will be found
A small bar of steel, a loadstone as well,
That points to the Pole and acts like a spell.

O is an Oyster, an expensive treat,
And if you buy natives you'll vouch they are sweet,
They are a dish for a King, they nourish the brain,
So if you would study, just try them again.

P stands for Port and when sailing at sea,
Whether close hauled or with the wind free;
Its the rule of the road and an excellent plan,
To use the port helm whenever you can.

Q will spell Quicksand, a most dangerous place,
That get lots of Captains in shocking disgrace;
Then look out for the Lightship and cast o'er the lead.
This hint then may save you from sorrow and dread.

R is the Rigging to hold up the mast,
When carrying sail before the rude blast;
So give her the sheet, 'tis a lowering sky,
To see bonny Kate to night we will try.

S stands for Stars, those heavenly flames,
Though few seamen boast of astrologers' fame,
They can point to Orion, or Saturn, or say,
Yonder the Pole Star, across Milkey Way.

T is for Tacking, get ready about,
Hard down with the helm the Skipper will shout;
Haul aft the jib sheet, your fore sail let fly,
There goes the Bold Admiral; to catch him we'll try.

U will spell Union Jack if you please,
A flag that we love to see float on the breeze,
Its an Englishman's hope where ere he may roam,
It reminds him of kindred and loved ones at home.

V stands for Vane, so trim and so smart,
'Tis a guide to the eye, oft the pride of his heart,
To hoist up gay colors of every hue,
With a smart, active, willing and wide-a-wake crew.

Windlas is spelt with a wi,
To heave in the cable, the bob stay and guy;
Ship your hand-spikes together, sing a cheery-like song
With a heart that is light and a arm that is strong.

X is a letter hard to bring in,
But every seaman should learn how to swim;
Then if by misfortune you fall in the sea,
What a blessing to you this lesson might be.

Y stands for Yarn, that an old tar can spin
To his shipmates below before they turn in,
Of adventures at sea, or freaks on the shore;
That will cause you to wonder or laugh till you roar.

Z will spell Zero, in Winter so cold,
But this letter reminds me my tale is now told,
Then cheer up my Fishermen friends on the main,
God guide you at sea, bring you safe home again.

During the herring boom of 1907, 2,500,000 barrels of fish (250,000 tons) were cured and exported, the main markets at the time being north Germany, Eastern Europe and Russia.

In 1912 52,000 lasts or cran (a last or cran being 13,200 fish and would weigh about 28 stones) were landed at Great Yarmouth.

During another boom in 1913 over 1,000 vessels were fishing out of Yarmouth, catching and selling herring to the value of about £1,000,000. On one day alone (23 October 1907) 80 million or 6,000 lasts of herrings were delivered to the fish wharfs of Yarmouth.

As the drifters pulled into the quay a swill of herring (a Yarmouth 'swill' was a basket containing 660 herrings) would be thrown onto the quayside where boys would carry them over to the bowler-hatted auctioneers as a sample so the catch would be ready for auction as soon as the boat had docked.

When the fishing fleet was docked at Great Yarmouth it was said you could walk from the town quayside to Gorleston on the bows of the boats.

The labours of the 6,000 Scottish 'fisher girls' appeared effortless and easy to the onlooker (until they tried it for themselves); one girl was timed and recorded as gutting fifty-seven herring in one minute!

The 'fisher girls' pay remained at 8*d* or 10*d* per barrel for years until 1936 when they went on strike to gain an extra 2*d* per barrel.

The herring industry was ruined by two world wars, overfishing (causing boom and bust prices), the decreasing demand for herring as public tastes changed and the diminishing of international custom. In addition to this, fishing vessels became increasingly expensive and unviable to run and all these factors combined led to a decline in this once massive industry. In 1968 only five Scottish drifters arrived in Great Yarmouth in what should have been high season, and in 1969 no Scottish boats came at all.

KING JOHN'S TREASURE

King John visited King's Lynn in 1216 and on his departure set out for Newark in Nottinghamshire via Wisbech, sending his chattels across the causeway over The Wash to arrive before him. Folklore tells of how the whole entourage was swept away by waves and engulfed by quicksands, never to be seen again. Treasure hunters are still searching for King John's treasure to this day!

VICTORIA COUNTY

In 1837 an extensive plan was drawn up for the reclamation of 150,000 acres of land from The Wash. This new land, planned to be about equal to the size of Rutland, was intended to be named in honour of the monarch, hence 'Victoria County'. The group of investors and engineers behind the scheme, which was estimated to cost £2 million, were headed by Lord William Bentinck and Sir William Ffolkes and included the eminent engineers Sir John Rennie and Robert Stephenson. The group became the Norfolk Estuary Company and were granted government approval for the project in 1848. Works officially commenced on the drainage project to create Victoria County on 8 November 1850 and work on the new drainage cut was progressing well until a dispute occurred between investors and the Wash ports opposed to the scheme. A legal wrangle ensued. The result was a financial drain and stress upon an already expensive project. The necessarily slow advancement of the work and the time and expense of getting the relevant acts through parliament as it progressed killed the dream. Over the ensuing years only 4,000 acres of The Wash were reclaimed by the Norfolk Estuary Company and about 3,500 by others.

LORD HIGH ADMIRAL OF THE WASH

Among the hereditary titles of the noble Le Strange family of Old Hunstanton is that of Lord High Admiral of The Wash, which gave them rights to the north-west Norfolk foreshore 'for as far as a man could ride out to sea at low tide and throw a javelin.' When Mercedes Gleitz, the cross-channel swimmer, set foot on the shore at Heacham on 29 June 1929 after becoming the first person to swim across The Wash (a marathon swim of 25 miles which she achieved in 13 hours and 17 minutes) she was greeted by the squire with the words 'You do understand, madam, that everything washed up on this beach belongs to me?'

PIERS

Cromer

The earliest pier, or rather a jetty, at Cromer was recorded as far back as 1391.

A 210ft-long jetty built of cast iron, made by Hase of Saxthorpe, was built at Cromer in 1822 but was totally destroyed in a storm in 1845.
.

A 240ft wooden jetty was built at Cromer in 1846 but this too was also damaged beyond repair during a storm in 1897.

In 1899 an Act was granted for the construction of a new pier at Cromer. The new pier, designed by engineer William Tregarthen Douglass, was opened on 8 June 1901 by Lord Claude Hamilton, Chairman of the Great Eastern Railway Company.

With the construction of the lifeboat station in 1923, Cromer Pier was extended to an overall length of 500ft.

Cromer Pier hosts the longest-running summertime pier show in Britain.

Cromer Pier has been badly damaged on three occasions: in 1940 when a hole was blown in it as an anti-invasion precaution, during the 1953 floods and in November 1993 when the 100-ton Tayjack 1 rig broke from its moorings in a severe storm and smashed through the pier causing a breach nearly 100ft long.

Britannia Pier, Great Yarmouth

Britannia Pier was first proposed in 1856 and work began in September 1857 with Mr A.W. Morant as the engineer.

It opened on 13 July 1858 and it originally measured 700ft long.

Its length was reduced on 25 October 1859 when during a severe storm the sloop *James and Jessie* crashed into the pier and severed the structure in two. Suffering further storm damage in 1868 it was demolished in 1899.

Work commenced on a new Britannia Pier on 13 December 1900. Designed by James and Arthur Mayoh, the 810ft pier was opened in 1901.

A temporary pavilion on the new pier was replaced with the Grand Pavilion, opened on 21 June 1902. This was, however, destroyed by fire on 22 December 1909.

A new Grand Pavilion was completed in 1910, but this too was burned down, this time by suffragettes on 17 April 1914. Within three months a replacement had been built and was opened on 27 July 1914.

Britannia Pier's Floral Hall Ballroom was opened in May 1928 but was wrecked by fire on 3 August 1932. A new Grand Ballroom opened in 1933. Known as the Ocean Ballroom from 1947, this was also destroyed by fire on 20 April 1954 along with the pavilion.

The pier was closed during the Second World War and reopened in 1947 after repairs. The present pavilion opened on 27 June 1958, but the ballroom was never replaced.

The Jetty, Great Yarmouth

A jetty has stood on this site for 450 years. It was rebuilt a number of times; the last one was erected in 1808.

Admiral Nelson landed at the jetty to great acclamation and celebrations after his victory at the Battle of Copenhagen in 1801.

The painter John Constable made three slightly different paintings of Yarmouth Jetty. One of them was acquired by his doctor, Robert Gooch, who, according to Constable, used to place it on the sofa while he breakfasted, as he used to say, 'on the seashore enjoying its breezes.'

Requiring £300,000 of repairs and after valiant attempts to save this historic jetty had been made by the Great Yarmouth and District Local History and Archaeological Society, Great Yarmouth Borough Council's development control committee voted by eight votes to two to pull down the jetty when they met on 18 January 2011.

Wellington Pier, Great Yarmouth

Wellington Pier was opened on 31 October 1853. The 700ft wooden structure designed by Mr P. Ashcroft cost £6,776 to build.

The pier was named in honour and memory of the Duke of Wellington, the victor of the Battle of Waterloo, prime minister and national hero who had died the previous year.

Great Yarmouth Borough Council bought Wellington Pier in 1900 for £1,250 and, under their ownership, the original wooden pier was reconstructed, a new pavilion built and opened on 13 July 1903 with pier gardens and a bandstand created on the southern side. They also acquired Winter Gardens for £2,400 from Torquay and brought to Yarmouth it was incorporated into the design of the pier.

The Pavilion Theatre was demolished just short of its 100th anniversary but has been replaced by another very similar structure. After extensive improvements and restoration work the pier and Winter Gardens are now open again.

Hunstanton Pier

Designed by one of the foremost pier engineers of his day, Mr J.W. Wilson, the 830ft long by 16ft wide Hunstanton Pier cost £2,000 and was opened on Easter Sunday in 1870.

The pavilion theatre suffered a severe fire on Saturday 10 June 1939. Two women, Miss Doris Bassford of Leicester and Miss Winifred Taylor of Wembley, were trapped at the end of the pier by the flames and had to jump into the sea to escape.

The pier was once graced with a small zoo, a roller-skating centre and a miniature steam railway that ran along its length.

The pier featured in the 1957 film *Barnacle Bill* starring Alec Guinness.

The majority of Hunstanton Pier was destroyed in a storm on 11 January 1978, leaving only the amusement arcade at the shoreward end; this too was destroyed in a fire in 2002.

LIGHTHOUSES

Hunstanton

A beacon or light has stood on St Edmund's Point for centuries. The old Chapel Light that stood on the site up to the 1830s contained the world's first parabolic reflector, built here in 1776. When the Chapel Light was sold to Trinity House in 1838 it was the last operational lighthouse in private hands. The present Hunstanton lighthouse building dates from 1840. In the 1880s it was claimed the light from atop the 50ft tower could be seen 16 miles out to sea. Hunstanton lighthouse was decommissioned and its lamp was taken down in 1921.

Cromer

Cromer's first 'light' was a brazier that burned on the top of the church tower. The first purpose-built lighthouse was one of five built along the coast by Sir John Clayton as an experiment. It is thought the Cromer light was never lit. Nathaniel Life and Edward Bowel lit the light of their lighthouse on Foulness for the first time in 1719. As the promontory of Foulness eroded, the old lighthouse became perilously close to the edge and a new lighthouse situated further inland was opened by Trinity House in 1833. The old Foulness lighthouse finally succumbed to a cliff fall on the night of 5/6 December 1866. At the zenith, the Cromer light produced a brightness of 100,000 candle power and it was claimed to be visible 23 miles out to sea. Graham Fearn, the last Cromer lighthouse keeper, stepped down in 1990.

Happisburgh

A matching pair of lights were established in Happisburgh by the Trinity Brethren in 1791. They were soon known as the 'High Light' on the cliff top and the 'Low Light' 20ft lower down the cliff. When the cliffs deteriorated the 'Low Light' became impractical so it was sold off by tender in the 1880s and demolished. The distinctive red and white stripes of Happisburgh Lighthouse were first painted in 1883. The tower is 85ft tall, putting the lantern at 135ft above sea level. The Happisburgh Light has a light characteristic of Fl (3) 30s (3 white flashes, repeated every 30 seconds) and has a range of 14 miles. Trinity House gave notice of closure of the lighthouse in 1987 but its fate has been saved by an energetic and enthusiastic group of local people and is today the only independently operated lighthouse in Great Britain. It is also the oldest working lighthouse in East Anglia.

Winterton

The first lighthouse was constructed between 1616 and 1618. Destroyed by fire, the Winterton Light was rebuilt in 1687 with an octagonal tower. It was purchased by Trinity House in 1837 and the premises were rebuilt three years later with a further rebuild in 1870.

Mr Squibb, the last full-time Winterton Lighthouse keeper, retired in 1919. Formally deactivated in 1921 the Winterton Light was sold off at the Star Hotel in Great Yarmouth in 1922 for £1,550.

Gorleston

The Gorleston Light was built in 1878 and stands 36ft high. It carries two lights; the rear light for the harbour entrance range (white light, 4 seconds on, 2 seconds off) is mounted on the tower with a focal plane of 23ft; a fixed red light is also displayed from the gallery with a focal plane of 66ft. It remains an active aid to navigation.

SMUGGLERS ALL

A smuggling boat was captured off Yarmouth by the Revenue cutter *Ranger* under the command of Captain Sayer in April 1821. About 400 tubs of Geneva and a quantity of dry goods were seized but the crew dived overboard and swam ashore to escape.

In February 1822 a smuggling boat landed 80 tubs of gin and brandy on Snettisham beach. The customs officers seized the cargo only to have some of it taken back by the smugglers and about 100 local people, some of them armed with bludgeons and shotguns. Two smugglers were wounded in the affray, but it appears that after retrieving what they could the smugglers and the villagers disappeared into the night.

The Customs Officers or 'Preventative Men' were disliked by many on the coast. In October 1822 the cutter *Ranger* went down off Happisburgh in the teeth of a gale. It was said 'the shrieks of the crew were heard distinctly from the shore', but no attempt was made to rescue them.

On 17 November 1832 Preventive Men at Brancaster seized a large tugboat containing 5,565lb of tobacco and 650 gallons of brandy and Geneva.

Lieutenant George Howes RN of the Weybourne Preventative Station and a party of coastguards under his command surprised a large number of smugglers at Cley on 26 February 1833. The smugglers put up a fearsome resistance and the coastguards were caused to discharge their weapons several times in self-defence. The haul they seized was, however, impressive: 127 half ankers of brandy and 3–4,000lb of manufactured tobacco.

THE BUSINESS OF BEACH COMPANIES

During the eighteenth and nineteenth centuries many settlements along our coastline had at least one beach company who would dash to their sheds, drag their boats into the water and would compete to get to any stricken vessel first. When the beachmen were accepted on board stricken vessels, handsome amounts could be negotiated from stranded captains. Terms would have to be formally agreed between the rescue boat coxswain and the ship's captain and 'mediated' by the beach company 'sea lawyer' (usually the most loquacious of the beachmen) before any rescue was undertaken!

FOR THOSE IN PERIL

The smaller eastern tower of Blakeney Church is said to have been used as a navigational aid and would be illuminated to indicate sufficient high water in the harbour for safe navigation. In 1830 Blakeney Church was still noted as an important sea mark. At the top of its 104ft tower flags would be hoisted in answer to vessels in distress. This mark was said to be seen at sea from the Dudgeon, or floating lights, some 21 miles away.

A Society for Recovering Drowned People was formed at Norwich in 1774.

The first purpose-built lifeboats in Norfolk were placed at Gorleston in 1802, followed by Cromer in 1805.

TO THE RESCUE.

The Norfolk Shipwreck Association was formed in 1823 to raise money to provide and maintain rescue vessels and the whole operation was taken over by the RNLI in 1857. The first statistics compiled in the two years after 1857, record ninety-five vessels were wrecked off Norfolk and 799 people rescued.

James Partridge Cubitt was, for many years during the nineteenth century, captain of the Bacton lifeboat crew. He received a number of medals and certificates for courageously saving lives on the Norfolk coast; on one occasion he even swam his horse out to a wreck and brought sailors he rescued to the shore hanging onto his stirrup leathers.

Captain George William Manby FRS, born 28 November 1765 in Denver, Norfolk, was serving as barrack master at Great Yarmouth when on 18 February 1807, as a helpless onlooker, he witnessed a naval ship, the *Snipe*, run aground 60 yards off the beach during a storm. Many people drowned, including French prisoners of war, women and children. Following this tragedy, Manby was inspired to revisit an experiment he had conducted as a youth in 1783, when he shot a mortar carrying a line over Downham church. After further experiments he invented the 'Manby Mortar' that could fire a thin rope from shore into the rigging of a ship in distress. A strong rope, attached to the thin one, could then be pulled aboard the ship. Manby's invention was officially adopted in 1814, and a series of mortar stations were established around the coast.

Happisburgh received its first lifeboat from the RNLI, a 32ft, ten-oared self-righting type named *Huddersfield* on 6 August 1866. The lifeboat was launched by a team of horses that would pull the boat on its carriage across the beach and into the water. For the first twenty-three years the horses used for every drill and service launch were supplied by Mr William Wilkins. When he died in 1890 a gratuity of £5 was granted to his widow in recognition of his services.

The Wells Lifeboat Disaster occurred on 29 October 1880. The *Eliza Adams* lifeboat, manned by thirteen men, capsized while on service. Eleven of the crew were drowned.

The first two Hunstanton lifeboats saved over 100 lives before 1900.

Over the course of sixty-one years preceding the closure of the Brancaster lifeboat station, their boat was launched thirty-two times and saved thirty-four lives.

The last boat to serve at Happisburgh RNLI station was the *Jacob and Rachel Valentine* which arrived in November 1907. She was sent by M&GN Railway to Stalham and then was conveyed by road to Happisburgh.

THE GREATEST LIFEBOATMAN

Henry Blogg (1876–1954), a born and bred Cromer man, was coxswain of the Cromer lifeboat for thirty-eight years and had a total of fifty-three years' service in the RNLI. He joined the Cromer lifeboat in 1894 when he was eighteen and made Coxswain by the age of thirty-three. During his years of service the Cromer lifeboat was launched 387 times and saved 873 lives. The actions of Henry Blogg and his crew rescuing men from stricken vessels such as *Fernebo*, *Monte Nervoso*, *Sepoy*, *Porthcawl* and *English Trader* have entered into lifeboat legend. One of his most significant actions, the *Sepoy*, demonstrates the bravery of the Cromer crew and the quick thinking, instinct and judgement of Henry Blogg. On 13 December 1933 the *Sepoy*, a 65-ton sailing barge, foundered just off Cromer and sank, the two-man crew climbed the rigging and lashed themselves to the mast. Henry Blogg dared to drive *HF Bailey* over the sunken decks of *Sepoy* – an act he had to repeat twice, snatching a crew member on each pass! With the rescue complete but the lifeboat short on fuel, there was no alternative but to drive for safety by beaching the boat on the Cromer shoreline. Each member of the crew of *HF Bailey* received RNLI vellums and Henry was awarded a second clasp for his RNLI silver medal. In total Henry Blogg was awarded the George Cross, the RNLI Gold medal (the 'Lifeboatman's VC') three times, three silver medals and the British Empire Medal. Henry respected the recognition he and his crews received but preferred to keep his medals in a box in the kitchen dresser than be seen wearing them.

THE LAST HERO OF THE *J.C. MADGE*

Jimmy 'Paris' West (1896–1987) was the last surviving member of the crew of the non-self-righting, pulling and sailing lifeboat *J.C. Madge*, which accomplished the most famous sea rescue in the history of Sheringham lifeboats. On 24 February 1916 the SS *Uller* of Bergen struck a sandbank in the teeth of a storm and made signals for assistance. Launching into a blizzard the *J.C. Madge* reached the *Uller* just inside the Blakeney Overfalls. It was found that she still had steam and could achieve half power, so the Sheringham men stood by in their open boat in swirling snow all through the night. In the morning the *Uller* began the voyage towards Grimsby towing the lifeboat behind. The crew of the *J.C. Madge* had a far from comfortable journey as they had to maintain constant efforts to avoid being flung onto the *Uller's* propeller (which was now half out of the sea, owing to the water in her damaged bow). It took two days for the vessels to reach the Humber and the lifeboatmen spent the night in Grimsby. A passing French steamer towed the lifeboat for some of the long journey home and the *J.C. Madge* finally returned to station at 6.00 p.m. on 28 February, four days after the first emergency signals had been spotted.

THE CAISTER LIFEBOAT DISASTER

The Caister Lifeboat Disaster occurred on 13 November 1901. After distress signals were sighted from a vessel on the Barber Sands, lifeboat *Beauchamp* managed to launch, in a second attempt, in horrific storm conditions that forced the boat back towards the beach. Striking the beach bow first about 50 yards from the launch point, the heavy sea struck the starboard quarter and capsized the boat, breaking off the masts and trapping the crew beneath. Despite the bravery of James and Frederick Haylett, who had been on the shore and managed to pull three men clear, the rest of the crew were lost. At the inquest retired coxswain James Haylett was asked why the crew had persisted in their rescue, he replied: 'They would never give up the ship. If they had to keep at it 'til now, they would have sailed about until daylight to help her. Going back is against the rules when we see distress signals like that.' In other words, Caister men never turn back, words that were to become the motto of the RNLI.

POPPYLAND

The Poppyland story began when Clement Scott published the first of his *Poppyland* columns written 'by a holidaymaker . . . at a farmhouse by the sea' in the *Daily Telegraph* on 30 August 1883. The sentimental stories of rural idylls and fields of swaying poppies on the north Norfolk coast appealed to the Victorian readership immediately. Thousands of visitors followed, all seeking this wonderful land between Sheringham and Sidestrand and found in the 'Garden of Sleep' by the ruined tower of Sidestrand church, perched so precariously near the cliff edge, and a fortune was to be made in souvenirs as diverse as china decorated with poppies, to books, postcards and even perfume. The area was eulogised by Clement Scott in his famous poem 'The Garden of Sleep':

> On the grass of the cliff, at the edge of the steep,
> God planted a garden - a garden of sleep!
> 'Neath the blue of sky, in the green of the corn,
> It is there that the regal red poppies are born!
> Brief days of desire, and long dreams of delight,

They are mine when Poppy-Land cometh in sight.
In music of distance, with eyes that are wet,
It is there I remember, and there I forget!
O! heart of my heart! where the poppies are born,
I am waiting for thee, in the hush of the corn.
Sleep! Sleep!
From the Cliff to the Deep!
Sleep, my Poppy-Land,
Sleep!

In my garden of sleep, where red poppies are spread,
I wait for the living, alone with the dead!
For a tower in ruins stands guard o'er the deep,
At whose feet are green graves of dear women asleep!
Did they love as I love, when they lived by the sea?
Did they wait as I wait, for the days that may be?
Was it hope or fulfilling that entered each breast,
Ere death gave release, and the poppies gave rest?
O! life of my life! on the cliffs by the sea,
By the graves in the grass, I am waiting for thee!
Sleep! Sleep!
In the Dews of the Deep!
Sleep, my Poppy-Land,
Sleep!

13

RIVERS, BROADS & MARSHLAND

WONDERFUL WATERWAYS

The Aylsham Navigation was opened in 1779 but was forced to close after the severe flooding of 1912 washed out the five locks between the current head of navigation on the River Bure at Coltishall and the town of Aylsham.

Norfolk's only canal, the North Walsham & Dilham, was formally opened on 29 August 1826. The final trading journey along it was made by the wherry *Ella* when she departed from Bacton Wood Staithe in 1934.

Norfolk wherries that plied our waterways and Broads as trade craft could carry around 25 tonnes of goods and were in service for around 200 years. Today, there are just eight wherries left.

There were once a number of ferries running across the rivers of the county including King's Lynn, Brundall, Buckenham, Horning, Stokesby and Pull's Ferry at Norwich, but only Reedham and Martham remain today.

The Thorpe 'water frolic' was instituted by Lieutenant-Colonel Harvey in 1821 and continued for many years in the nineteenth century. Sailing matches and rowing matches were held, all contending for silver cups. At these events it was recorded 'the banks of the Yare were thronged with genteel company' often numbering upwards of 10,000.

TEN LESSER-KNOWN RIVERS OF NORFOLK

The River Ainse (or Eyn): a tributary of the River Wensum that merges with it at Lenwade.

The River Cong rises on the Hillington side of Congham – it is just 1.5 miles long.

The River Gadder: A tributary of the River Wissey that rises at Cockley Cley.

The River Hor: Rises from a spring in St Margaret's churchyard in Felthorpe, runs through Horsham St Faith and merges with the River Bure.

The River Mun: Rising in the parish of Northrepps, the Mun flows through Gimingham and runs into the North Sea at Mundesley.

The River Tat: A tributary of the River Wensum. Its source is on Syderstone Common, just north of the village of Tattersett.

The River Tiffey: A tributary of the Yare, it rises at Hethel then flows through Wymondham, Kimberley, Carlton Forehoe, Wramplingham and Barford and joins the River Yare at Swan's Harbour.

The River Tud: A tributary of the River Wensum. Its source is just south of East Dereham and it flows in an easterly direction to its confluence with the Wensum below Hellesdon Mill.

The River Wissey: Rises near Bradenham and joins the Great Ouse at Fordham.

The River Ingol: Has its source to the west of Shernbourne and flows towards Snettisham and Ingoldisthorpe and joins The Wash at Wolferton Creek.

BROADLAND BANTER

The Norfolk Broads are not a natural phenomenon but flooded medieval peat workings.

The Norfolk and Suffolk Broads are Britain's largest protected wetland and the third largest waterways with the status of a national park.

The Broads have a total length of about 188 miles, mostly in the county of Norfolk.

Just over 77 square miles of the Broads are navigable, covering a total of seven rivers and sixty-three Broads.

There are forty-one Broads in Norfolk.

The largest Broad is Hickling Broad that covers 141 hectares.

Horsey Mere is the only Broad known as a mere.

In the 1880s there were 240 drainage mills dotted throughout the Broads, 74 remain today but many of them are derelict.

About 130,000 bundles of Norfolk Reed for thatching are harvested on the Broads every year.

Sedge, used to form the ridge or cap on thatched roofs, is harvested on the Broads in the summer months.

John Loynes founded the first boat hire company on the Broads in 1878. Today, there are about 2,000 hire and 11,000 private craft on the Broads.

COYPU

The first coypu were introduced from South American farms into the Broadland area for fur production in 1929. During the Second World War many coypu were released from fur farms into the countryside without thinking what damage they may cause upon it. By the early 1960s the problem had become so bad that a coypu control committee was set up by government. Throughout the 1970s coypu damage to banks, reed beds and crops on adjoining farmland escalated to became a serious problem. The systematic eradication of the coypu began in 1981 and the last of them were exterminated from the Norfolk Broads in 1989.

MARSHLAND MEANDERINGS

Dutch engineer Cornelius Vermuyden built the first Denver sluice in 1651 as part of drainage scheme for the Fens owned by the Duke of Bedford.

In 1774 George Walpole, 3rd Earl of Orford, set out with a fleet of nine boats to explore the Fens with the same sense of adventure one may have recorded for a voyage and exploration of darkest Africa.

The potential of man-made land reclamation of the Fens on the Norfolk and Cambridgeshire borders reached its height in the seventeenth century. The lands of the Duke of Bedford between Earith in Cambridgeshire and Salters Lode were drained according to the plans and methods of the Dutch engineer Vermuyden in 1637, which included the construction of the New Bedford River (the Hundred Foot Drain) and the first Denver Sluice.

When Marshland free bridge and causeway was opened in August 1822, after a congratulatory speech by Mr Hoseason, a lunch was provided for 200 people at the expense of the directors. A further dinner was given that same evening at the Freemason's Tavern and on Mr Goddard's marshes at West Lynn a fair for stock was held for the first time. A sheep was roasted and several barrels worth of beer were given away.

COMPLEAT ANGLERS

In 1811 two anglers fishing near Buckenham Ferry between the hours of 6.00 a.m. and 5.00 p.m. caught 132lb of perch, bream and roach.

In 1819 a salmon measuring 48in in length, 23in in girth and weighing 33lb was caught at the New Mills, Norwich.

A sturgeon measuring 6ft 2in, 3ft 6in in girth and weighing 15 stone 3lb was shot in the River Wissey near Hilgay Bridge in May 1850. It was all the more remarkable that the fish should be so far up the river when it was considered it would have had to pass through a number of sluices to get there.

A porpoise weighing over 1cwt was caught near the free staithe at West Somerton, some 25 miles from the sea, in September 1838.

A common bream weighing a record-breaking 18lb 12oz was caught in Bawburgh Lakes in 2001.

A pike weighing 45lb 8oz was caught by John Goble on the Norfolk Broads in March 2009.

The current carp record was set in 2010 on the Broadwing Lake, Taswood Lakes, where a Ghost Carp named the 'lady of the lake' was caught that weighed in at 41lb 3oz.

John 'Watto' Watson, one of the country's foremost pike fishermen and one of the sport's most colourful characters, author of *A Piker's Progress* and numerous articles about the art of fishing, has lived in Norfolk for many years.

John Wilson MBE, voted 'the greatest angler of all time' in a 2004 poll by readers of the *Angling Times*, is well known for his television programmes and many books on angling. He has resided in Norfolk for many years and currently lives at Great Witchingham.

14

SENSE OF PLACE

A SENSE OF IDENTITY

There are a plethora of old local nicknames for people originating from particular villages – some of them are retained with great pride to this day.

Cromer Crabs
Runton Dabs
Bessingham Bannocks
Cley Geese
Cockthorpe Slows (blind worms)
Baconsthorpe Strippers
Langham Fairmaids or Lions
Stiffkey or Stewkey Blues
Binham Bulls
Stiffkey Trolls
Blickling Flats
Marsham Peewits
Holt Owls or Know-alls
Swaffham Pedlars
Gorleston Jews
Reedham Rats
Cantley Cats
Moulton Mules
Freethorpe Fools

Sheringham Shannocks or Ladies
Beeston Babies
Weybourne Witches
Salthouse Ditches
Glandford Nobles
Gresham Mites
Blakeney Bulldogs
Morston Doddermen (also
    recorded as Dodmen – snails)
Wells Bitefingers
Aylsham Fliers
Hevingham Liars
Norwich Joes or Canaries
Yarmouth Bloaters
Halvergate Hares
Southwood Swine
Acles Asses
Beighton Bears

NORFOLK'S STRANGEST NAMES

Mahershallalashbaz Tuck   (East Dereham, 1866)
The Revd Lawrence Strongitharm   (Norwich, 1827)
John Wanker   (King's Lynn, 1587)
Cockle Cadywold   (Norwich, 1800)
Haseleys Peascod   (Norfolk Poll Book, 1802)

Christmas Bear	(Norwich, 1873)
Absolom Pattle	(Worstead, 1930)
Nebuchadnezzar Carr	(Downham Market, 1871)
Grimmer Cock	(Hockwold, 1861)
Zebulon Rouse	(Booton, 1851)
Knipe Gobbett	(Norwich, 1771)
Kerenhappuck Cockett	(Norwich, 1873)
William Worf	(East Walton, 1820)
William Glasscock	(Stow Bardolph, 1891)
Hamo Garlicman	(Norwich, 1355)
Phoebe Winkle	(Norwich, 1871)
Florence Bollock	(Diss, 1864)
Rachel Shite	(Norwich, 1841)
John Sucker	(Norwich, 1836)
Mary Bummer	(King's Lynn, 1841)
Joseph Hugman	(Norwich, 1782)
John Seapey	(Snettisham, 1890)

There was even a Gotobed family living at Little Snoring

NORFOLK ENIGMAS

Roys of Wroxham is actually in Hoveton.

Bressingham is near Diss but Bessingham is in North Norfolk.

Salthouse is in North Norfolk but Salhouse is near Norwich.

Beeston is also known as Beeston All Saints or Beeston-next-Mileham; there are also Beeston Regis, Beeston St Andrew, Beeston St Lawrence and Beeston with Bittering in other quite separate parts of the county.

Fleggburgh and Burgh St Margaret is the same place.

Framingham Earl and Framingham Pigot are close together and can also be found recorded as Framlingham Earl and Framlingham Pigot. To confuse matters further, Framlingham is miles away in Suffolk.

Happisburgh is pronounced Haisbrugh but then, a short distance out to sea, there are the Haisborough Sands.

There is a railway signal-box in Happisburgh but there was never a railway there.

Oxburgh Hall is in Oxborough, Norfolk.

North and South Walsham are miles apart.

The Heigham, as in Potter Heigham or Heigham in Norwich, is pronounced by some as 'Higham' but by others as 'Ham'. Locals in Potter Heigham avoid any discrepancies by referring to their home as simply 'Potter'.

Little Hautbois is pronounced Little Hobbus, Northrepps is Nodrupps, Shotesham is Shottsum and Hindolveston is known to locals as Hindol.

Why is there a dual carriageway near Tunstead?

THASS A RUMMUN!

Here's a collection of Norfolk words and phrases, but please note, because these are colloquialisms the written spelling of these words may vary across the county:

Thass a rummun – An exclamation of surprise or disbelief
Bor – A neighbour or friend, can be male or female
Mawther – A woman
Squit – nonsense
Mardle – To have a leisurely and enjoyable conversation
My hat an' 'onour – A statement of earnest surprise
Bishy-barney-bee – A ladybird
Dickey – A donkey
She mobbed me – She fussed me
Dwile – A floor cloth
That put me in the mind of – That reminds me of
Mawkin – A scarecrow
Me ole bewty – A fond term of friendship
Teeter-ma-torter – A see-saw
Honey Cart – A sewage cart or truck
Thass black over Will's mother's – Bad weather is on the way
Keep yew a' troshin – Keep up the good work
Woss gorn on? – What is happening?
Hold yew hard – Hang on a minute
Titty-Totty – A small thing, could be a person but normally an object
Fare thee well together – Goodbye

15

ON THIS DAY

JANUARY

1 January 1931 Norwich City Police commenced motor police patrols under the new Road Traffic Act.

2 January 1874 Susannah Steavenson died at Neal's Square, St Benedict's Church Alley, Norwich in her 105th year.

3 January 1837 Murder of Hannah Mansfield 'the Denver Fortune Teller'. Her killers, John Varnham, John Smith and George Timms, were apprehended, found guilty and executed at Norwich on 29 April 1837.

4 January 1857 A violent gale off Yarmouth drove several ships ashore leaving the beach a melancholy sight.

5 January 1852 Johnson Jex, a brilliant man, blacksmith and watch maker, died at Letheringsett.

6 January 1945 Norwich honoured the Royal Norfolk Regiment by granting it the privilege of marching through the city with colours flying, band playing and bayonets fixed.

7 January 1814 At the burial of coachman Benjamin Edwards at Blickling, a close friend doused the lid of the coffin with rum exclaiming, 'I have performed my promise as I am sure he would have done had I gone first.'

8 January 1846 The last horse-drawn mail coach ran from Norwich to London.

9 January 1824 John Thurtell, son of a Norwich Mayor, was hanged at Hertford for the murder of William Weare. The case revolved around gambling debts and was a sensation in its day with numerous supplements, broadsides and books published about it.

10 January 1891 An ice carnival took place on Diss Mere. The performers and spectators numbered 5,000.

11 January 1978 Storms reduced the majority of the 830ft Hunstanton pier to scrap metal; it has not been rebuilt.

12 January 1616 Mary Smith burned at the stake in the Tuesday Market Place, King's Lynn.

13 January 1830 During a time of unrest among the weavers of Norwich, sulphuric acid was thrown in the face of John Wright, one of the principle master manufacturers in the city, on St Faith's Lane.

14 January 1887 Socialists Mowbray and Henderson fired up a crowd of unemployed workmen in Norwich Market Place to procure food, themselves causing a riot, and a number of shops were attacked.

15 January 1869 A trout weighing 15lb was captured in a drop net near the New Mills, Norwich.

16 January 1913 Sexton's Shoe factory on Fishergate, Norwich, was destroyed by fire.

17 January 1920 Princess Mary presided at a rally of 2,000 Norfolk Girl Guides at St Andrew's Hall, Norwich.

18 January 1828 A bodysnatcher was shot attempting to disinter the body of James Howlett at Bacton. Despite being badly wounded the resurrection man ran off and disappeared into the darkness.

19 January 1915 The first bombs dropped by a Zeppelin in an offensive raid over Great Britain were dropped on Norfolk.

20 January 1936 HM King George V died at Sandringham House aged seventy.

21 January 1860 A 'Spring Heel'd Jack' caused mischief and stirred up fear in Southtown, Great Yarmouth.

22 January 1927 A telephone service between the USA and Norfolk opened and the first messages were transmitted.

23 January 1963 Horstead Mill, the last mill on the Bure and one of the biggest, best known and most photographed mills in the county, was gutted by fire.

24 January 1819 Madame Tussaud's collection, including the wax casts she had taken from the nobility of France after they were guillotined, were exhibited at the Angel Inn, Norwich.

25 January 1925 Queen Mary attended Norwich Cathedral for the rededication of the Bishop's throne.

26 January 1932 Water and sewage schemes opened at Wymondham.

27 January 1547 The order was given for the execution of Thomas Howard, 3rd Duke of Norfolk, the next day. The king died during the night and his order was not carried out.

28 January 1837 A severe influenza epidemic swept the county, a number of fatalities were recorded.

29 January 1737 Thomas 'Tom' Paine, author of *The Rights of Man*, and one of the founding fathers of the United States of America, was born at Thetford.

30 January 1908 Richard Hearne OBE, actor, comedian, producer and writer best known for his character Mr Pastry, was born on Lady Lane, Norwich.

31 January 1949 Royal Links Hotel at Cromer gutted by fire.

FEBRUARY

1 February 1953 The dawn over the county revealed scenes of devastation along the coast from the worst North Sea surge on record. A total of 307 people lost their lives along the East Coast.

2 February 1570 A great flood washed away Fyebridge on the north side of Norwich.

3 February 1839 A prizefight was staged on Costessey Common between Rix and Clarke. Sixty-three rounds were fought over 1 hour and 20 minutes. Rix was the victor.

4 February 1875 Fire at Norwich city gaol ruined the treadmill house.

5 February 1856 Jenny Lind sang a performance of 'The Messiah' at St Andrew's Hall, Norwich.

6 February 1952 HM King George VI died at Sandringham House aged fifty-six.

7 February 1910 Dr E.E. Blyth was created first Lord Mayor of Norwich.

8 February 1864 John Bennett, the last resident of Norwich of the 'old school' to wear a pigtail, died on this day aged ninety-one.

9 February 1805 A woman who had eloped from Kent with a horse dealer was found by her husband at a house in St Peter Mancroft.

The horse dealer offered to buy the woman, so a halter was placed around her neck, she was taken to Norwich Market Place and sold to him for £5.

10 February 1941 A rail crash took place at Brentwood in Essex between the Norwich Express and a train bound for Southend. Six people were killed and twenty-one injured.

11 February 1885 Notorious fraudster Arthur Orton 'The Tichborne Claimant' came to Norwich on this day with Sanger's Circus. Orton gained notoriety when he attempted to impersonate the lost son of the Dowager Lady Henriette Tichborne and lay claim to the family fortune. Exposed as an impostor he was sent to prison and having served fourteen years for his crime was released and began a tour exhibiting himself as a curiosity.

12 February 1948 New synagogue was consecrated at Norwich

13 February 1864 An announcement was made that a new religious order or brotherhood was being raised in Norwich. Shortly afterwards five brethren, led by the notorious Brother Ignatius, took up residence in their 'monastery' on Elm Hill.

14 February 1859 Phineas T. Barnum, the celebrated showman, delivered a lecture at St Andrew's Hall, Norwich, on 'Money-making and the Art of Humbug'.

15 February 1821 The Morning Star coach overturned at Scole Inn, and one passenger, a Mr Butterfield of Leeds, later died of his injuries.

16 February 1863 Prof. J.H. Pepper lectured at Noverre's Rooms, Norwich, on optical illusions and for the first time in the city, exhibited his famous illusion 'Pepper's Ghost'.

17 February 1947 In the month when Norfolk experienced the worst snowfall for fifty years a constant frost was recorded in Norwich for 198 hours.

18 February 1911 The Picture House Cinematograph Theatre opened on the Haymarket, Norwich.

19 February 1840 Richard Pattle of Rudham died in his 108th year. He was a poor but honest man who earned his bread by the sweat of his brow.

20 February 1819 Mrs Elizabeth Wells, wife of Robert Wells of Gressenhall gave birth to live quads – three boys and a girl.

21 February 1947 Skating was possible on the river between Oulton and Beccles for the first time since 1894.

22 February 1908 Sir John Mills, actor who made more than 120 films over seven decades, was born at Watts Naval School, North Elmham.

23 February 1843 A collision took place between the Norwich to London coach and a brewer's dray at Tasburgh. The guard was killed outright and coachman Thomas Wiggins was severely injured.

24 February 1939 The Northern Lights were seen over Norfolk.

25 February 1847 Work commenced on the Norwich extension of the Ipswich and Bury Extension Railway.

26 February 1833 An affray took place between coastguards under Lt George Howes RN and a large armed party of smugglers at Cley.

27 February 2008 An earthquake of 5.2 on the Richter scale and lasting 10 seconds rocked folks in their beds at approximately 1.00 a.m.

28 February 1839 Smallpox was prevalent in Norwich; over 100 had died during the month.

29 February 1860 The county cleared up after a severe gale, that raged across the region the previous day, abated. Great damage was inflicted along the coast, numerous houses and buildings were damaged inland, many trees were uprooted and several lives had been lost.

MARCH

1 March 1836 The new police were on duty for the first time in Norwich.

2 March 1839 Smallpox was reported to be very prevalent in Norwich. Within the preceding month 100 persons had died of the disease in the city.

3 March 1988 An Eastern Counties double-decker bus fell into an old chalk mine tunnel that opened up on Earlham Road.

4 March 1642 William Goslyn, Mayor of Norwich, was taken to Cambridge and confined for three months for refusing to confirm the orders of parliament.

5 March 1694 The death of Henry Wharton, distinguished theologian and scholar, formerly a student at the Paston School, North Walsham. He was buried at Westminster Abbey.

6 March 1880 A disastrous fire struck in a range of shops and private houses at Old Buckenham causing damages in excess of £3,000.

7 March 1842 Norwich weavers commenced a strike to enforce a return to the scheduled prices paid in 1836.

8 March 1823 Messrs Marshalls' panorama of the Battle of Trafalgar and the death of Nelson exhibited at Norwich.

9 March 1851 A fire broke out at the offices of the *Norwich Mercury* on Castle Street, Norwich. The roof fell in on the compositor's room and most of the cases of type were destroyed.

10 March 1863 A roast beef feast held in East Dereham for over 2,000 poor people was held to mark the wedding of the Prince of Wales.

11 March 1944 Keith Skipper MBE, DL, journalist, author and Norfolk champion, was born at Beeston-next-Mileham

12 March 1869 A race was staged between Joseph Tuck, a pedestrian, of Little Snoring and a trotting pony belonging to Mr Gutteridge over 500 yards for £40. Tuck passed over the finish line 30 yards ahead of the pony.

13 March 1866 A boiler explosion took place at Arnold & Wyatt's brewery on St Margaret's Plain, Norwich. Engine driver William Whitworth was killed in the blast 'his body being hurled into the beck containing six quarters of boiling wort.'

14 March 1927 The Round Table was founded by Eminio William Louis Marchesi at Suckling House, Norwich.

15 March 1819 Captain Manby exhibited his new invention, a fire cart operated by one man, to the Mayor and Corporation of Great Yarmouth.

16 March 1819 The foundation stone of Prince's Street Chapel, Norwich, was laid by the Revd John Alexander.

17 March 1828 The death of Sir James Edward Smith MD, botanist, founder and first President of the Linnaean Society. He had been born at Norwich in 1759.

18 March 1865 Mary Doughty died at North Walsham aged 101.

19 March 1868 The boiler of a steam engine exploded while working in a field near Watlington station killing five and injuring seven others, two of whom died the following day.

20 March 1884 Oscar Wilde lectured to a large audience in the Assembly Room, Agricultural Hall, Norwich, on the subject of 'The House Beautiful'.

21 March 1897 Mark Knights, antiquarian, author of *Highways and Byways of Norwich* and chief reporter of the *Eastern Daily Press* died of asphyxiation caused by an escape of gas in his bedroom at the Cheshire Cheese Hotel, Surrey Street, Strand, London.

22 March 1947 Southery Fen flooded and was under 2ft of water.

23 March 1842 Disturbances at Lynn took place owing to a reduction of wages of coal porters and sailors.

24 March 1933 Sprowston Mill, otherwise known as Crome's Mill, was destroyed by fire.

25 March 1936 3,000 women gathered at Norwich Cathedral for a Mothers' Union Festival.

26 March 1916 Bill Edrich DFC, distinguished cricketer who played for Middlesex, MCC, Norfolk and England, was born at Lingwood.

27 March 1929 Blyth Secondary School for Girls opened at New Catton.

28 March 1851 At the Norfolk Assizes George Baldry was found guilty of the murder of Caroline Watts at Thurlton by striking her on the head with a hammer. His death sentence was commuted to transportation for life.

29 March 1867 Charles Dickens appeared at St Andrew's Hall, Norwich, where he read *Dr Marigold* and the trial scene from *The Pickwick Papers* before a large audience.

30 March 1820 Anna Sewell, best known as the author of the classic novel *Black Beauty*, was born at Great Yarmouth.

31 March 1816 The Revd Valentine Lumley Barnard, rector of Stockton, died while delivering a sermon from Hales Church.

APRIL

1 April 1875 The Yarmouth and Gorleston tramway was formally opened by the Mayor of Yarmouth.

2 April 1823 Mad Dogs in Norwich. Owners were requested to keep their pets confined lest they run the risk of them being bitten by the mad dogs or shot as one.

3 April 1370 Henry Despenser was appointed Bishop of Norwich.

4 April 1853 A severe fire broke out at Hunstanton Hall. Many contents, including the bed slept in by Elizabeth I, were saved, but the hall suffered damage estimated at £10,000.

5 April 1832 The first outbreak of cholera in Norfolk during the nineteenth century broke out at Stow Bridge. In the following two months thirty-three cases were reported, thirteen of them proving fatal.

6 April 1918 Norwich Tank Week raised £1,057,382 for War Bonds.

7 April 1828 Entertainer Ching Lao Lauro received what was described as 'the worst review in the history of performance in Norwich.'

8 April 1831 Jem Mace, 'The Norfolk Gypsy', the first world boxing champion and one of the greatest boxers of all time, was born at Beeston.

9 April 1910 The Theatre de Luxe cinematograph show opened in St Andrew's Street, Norwich.

10 April 1862 Jenny Lind appeared at a concert given at St Andrew's Hall, Norwich.

11 April 1846 Samuel Yarham, having been found guilty of the murder of Harriet Candler at Great Yarmouth, was executed outside Norwich Castle before 30,000 spectators.

12 April 1995 The Assembly House, Norwich, burned down but was restored in a £385,000 project.

13 April 1856 A serious gas explosion took place at Gurney's Bank, Norwich, after a clerk named Utting, smelling the escape of gas, went to investigate with a lighted candle.

14 April 1873 The foundation stone of the Norfolk County School at North Elmham was laid by HRH the Prince of Wales.

15 April 1831 Sir Thomas Fowell Buxton of Overstrand made a resolution in House of Commons to abolish slavery.

16 April 1925 A battered R33 airship limped back to Pulham after gale force winds tore it from its mooring mast. The gallant crew only regained control when the airship had been blown out across the North Sea to the Dutch coast but they managed to bring it back. All crew were presented with watches by the king and Flight Sergeant 'Sky' Hunt was awarded the Air Force Medal.

17 April 1914 Britannia Pier, Great Yarmouth, burned down in a fire started by militant suffragettes.

18 April 1829 Three men were executed on Norwich Castle Hill – John Wood and Thomas Butler for stealing sheep and Richard Everitt for horse stealing.

19 April 1917 Heavy losses were suffered by the men of the 4th and 5th Battalions, the Norfolk Regiment (T.F.) at the Second Battle of Gaza.

20 April 1869 The execution of William Sheward took place at Norwich city gaol for the murder of his wife. He had killed his wife and distributed her body parts around the city. Her remains were unidentified and Sheward had literally got away with murder but troubled by his deed over the ensuing years, he finally confessed to the crime eighteen years later.

21 April 1888 A party of sixty emigrants from parishes around Diss left for Canada.

22 April 1883 A porpoise, brought up on a flood tide, was killed in the Yare at Buckenham Ferry.

23 April 1648 'The Great Blowe' – the largest explosion in the English Civil War – occurred when the parliamentary committee armoury exploded during a riot in Norwich.

24 April 1819 Master Sewell, 'the Lincolnshire gigantic youth' who weighed 18 stone at the age of thirteen, and Miss Eleanor Fitzjohn 'Queen of the Dwarfs' (for she was only 30in tall) were exhibited at the Two-Necked Swan, Market Place, Norwich.

25 April 1828 A whirlwind at Gresham roared across the village for just three minutes but ruined poor William Watts by tearing not only the sails but the whole fabric of the his windmill from its post, wrecking it in the process.

26 April 1941 The worst loss of life in Norfolk during a single bombing incident occurred when a bomb dropped on the packed Horning Ferry pub. Twenty-one lives were lost and several more individuals were injured.

27 April 1942 First night of the 'Baedeker Blitz' on Norwich took place. 50 tons of bombs dropped, causing 600 casualties including 162 deaths.

28 April 1810 A rare fish called the Opah or King Fish, more familiar to Icelandic waters, was found on Mundesley beach.

29 April 1942 On the second night of the 'Baedeker Blitz' 45 tons of high explosive incendiaries dropped on Norwich; 69 people were killed and 89 seriously injured.

30 April 1932 The municipal golf course at Earlham opened by the Lord Mayor.

MAY

1 May 1886 A new station designed by Mr J. Wilson, erected by the Great Eastern Railway at Thorpe, Norwich, was opened for inspection. It had cost £60,000, a massive sum of money in its day.

2 May 1844 Great Yarmouth suspension bridge collapsed, causing the death of 130 men, women and children.

3 May 1862 Mother of twenty-two children, Phoebe Clayburn, died at Rackheath aged 103.

4 May 1970 Fire raged in three separate locations: Blackborough End near King's Lynn, at Kelling and over 80 acres of heath at Dersingham.

5 May 1803 Press gangs claiming unwilling recruits for the Royal Navy were active in Great Yarmouth.

6 May 1935 King George V Jubilee celebrations in the city – 'Norwich goes gay'.

7 May 1927 Viscount Allenby unveils a memorial to fallen men of the Norfolk Regiment on the Mount of Olives, Palestine.

8 May 1945 VE Day celebrations took place across the county. 5,000 marched through the streets of Norwich to the service at the cathedral.

9 May 1825 The Norwich Museum was opened at a house in the Upper Haymarket.

10 May 1936 King's Lynn Theatre Royal burned to the ground.

11 May 1943 Twenty FW 190s appeared over Great Yarmouth at 8.45 a.m. A company of 30 ATS girls marching to their billet at Sefton House on North Drive ran to their hostel for cover, moments later a bomb was dropped on the building. A total of twenty-six girls lost their lives. This is regarded as one of the worst instances of loss of life among female service personnel during the Second World War.

12 May 1955 The speaking clock was available to Norwich telephone users for the first time.

13 May 1821 Christopher Allcock died at Lyng, aged ninety-one. He had served in the first draft of the Norfolk Militia called out in 1759 and had kept his old military coat so it might serve him as a shroud.

14 May 1829 The body of Lorina Gooderham was found murdered on Brome Lane, Diss. The crime remains unsolved.

15 May 1923 The Old Norwich Bridewell was presented to the city by Mr H.N. Holmes.

16 May 1890 William Gladstone visited Norwich. Arriving at Thorpe station, he was entertained at Carrow Abbey and he gave an address in the evening at a vast meeting at the Agricultural Hall.

17 May 1729 Samuel Clarke, the Norwich-born philosopher who adopted Newton's theories of physics, died.

18 May 1950 Church of St Paul, Hellesdon, was dedicated and became the first new church to be opened in the diocese since the Second World War.

19 May 1850 Lieutenant John Allen, commander of the revenue cutter *Prince of Wales*, boarded the *Sea Flower* of Hull off Happisburgh and found it laden with 122 50lb bales of tobacco with a potential duty of £900. Both vessel and cargo were confiscated.

20 May 1853 No prisoners were held in Lynn Gaol, so the mayor entertained the whole police force and borough officials to a dinner there, served within the walls.

21 May 1872 Captain Bates, 'The Kentucky Giant', and Chrissie Millie, the 'Two-Headed Nightingale', appeared at the Lecture Hall, St Andrew's, Norwich.

22 May 1882 William George Abigail was executed at Norwich Castle for the murder of Jane 'Jennie' Plunkett.

23 May 1852 A serious fire took place at the Norfolk Hotel, Norwich. The roof was entirely consumed and a number of rooms destroyed.

24 May 1855 Great Yarmouth waterworks were opened with great public festivity.

25 May 1940 The first bombs to be dropped on the county during the Second World War landed to the north-east of RAF West Raynham shortly after midnight.

26 May 1863 Entertainers Charles Marsh and Henry Wharton attempted to climb Nelson's Monument at Great Yarmouth. Both succeeded but Marsh slipped on the way down and fell 144ft to his death.

27 May 1828 The Thames steam packet *Capt. John Morley* was the first seaborne vessel to travel from London to Norwich port direct. The duration of her voyage was 28 hours.

28 May 1972 Neil R. Storey, Norfolk historian and author, was born at Norwich.

29 May 1929 Revd Samuel F. Leighton Green MC and Bar, the author of *The Happy Padre*, was Rector of Mundesley Church from 1921 until his death on this day.

30 May 1929 The death of Harry Moulton (aged seventy-three), the last Norwich Bellman.

31 May 1882 The new Town Hall for Great Yarmouth was opened by HRH the Prince of Wales.

JUNE

1 June 1939 Railway disaster at Hilgay. Four people were killed and eight injured when the Hunstanton to London Express was derailed by a lorry.

2 June 1895 A serious fire occurred on board the *Jenny Lind* steamboat at Foundry Bridge, Norwich.

3 June 1864 William Johnson Fox, many years MP for Oldham, popularly known as 'The Norwich Weaver Boy', died in his seventy-eighth year.

4 June 1887 Queen Kapiolani, heiress presumptive to the Hawaiian throne, was entertained at Rackheath Hall.

5 June 1879 A passenger train from Norwich crashed through the buffer stops colliding with the porter's room and lavatories at Wells station. A young man named James Cook was killed.

6 June 1944 Men of the 1st Battalion, the Royal Norfolk Regiment made a successful landing on Queen Red Sector of Sword Beach on D-Day.

7 June 1911 New golf links were formally opened at Eaton, Norwich.

8 June 1901 Cromer pier was opened by Lord Claude Hamilton, Chairman of the Great Eastern Railway Company.

9 June 1933 Kett's Oak on Wymondham Road was filled with 2 tons of concrete to preserve it from further decay.

10 June 1939 Hunstanton Pier Pavilion was destroyed by fire.

11 June 1923 Scolt Head Island was formally handed over to the National Trust by public subscription.

12 June 1827 A weavers' riot took place in Norwich. A mounted charge to disperse the crowd and street patrols were carried out by the Norwich Light Horse Volunteers.

13 June 1802 Author Harriet Martineau was born in Norwich. It was said of her, 'Although she was not a great she was a most industrious writer and thoroughly earnest in whatever she undertook.'

14 June 1645 Melton Constable-born Royalist supporter Jacob Astley (1st Baron Asley of Reading), commanded the main body of foot infantry at Battle of Naseby.

15 June 1865 The first two-day show of the Norfolk Agricultural Association commenced on Chapel Field, Norwich.

16 June 1843 For nearly three hours the sun was observed to be surrounded by a bright and beautiful halo, while several others appeared in its vicinity, intersecting the main one in several directions.

17 June 1879 The foundation stone of the new Norfolk and Norwich Hospital was laid by HRH the Prince of Wales.

18 June 1895 The old Tolhouse at Great Yarmouth was opened as a museum.

19 June 1947 The artist Sir Alfred Munnings was admitted as an Honorary Freeman of Norwich.

20 June 1897 Queen Victoria's Diamond Jubilee took place with street parties and celebratory events across the county.

21 June 1738 Death of Norfolk agriculturalist Viscount Charles 'Turnip' Townshend of Raynham Hall.

22 June 1757 Captain George Vancouver was born in New Conduit Street, King's Lynn.

23 June 1822 The tower of Happisburgh church was considerably damaged by lightning during a great storm over the county.

24 June 1912 The training brig *Lord Nelson* was formally dedicated at Norwich.

25 June 1600 Much of North Walsham, including the old Market Cross, was burned down in the space of about two hours.

26 June 1381 The defeat of the rebels of the Peasants' Revolt by Bishop Henry Despenser and his troops took place at North Walsham.

27 June 1923 Edward, Prince of Wales, opened the new Carrow Bridge, Norwich.

28 June 1853 Spiritualism was introduced to Norwich when the first séance was held at St Andrew's Hall by Mr King.

29 June 1939 Norfolk County Cricket Club drew with the West Indies at Lakenham.

30 June 1883 A disastrous thunderstorm occurred at Norwich, with several low-lying streets flooded. A man was killed when he was struck by lightning near Unthank Road; while another suffered the same fate at Earlham.

JULY

1 July 1952 Chris Sugden, Norfolk humorist, best known for his portrayal of fictional folk singer Sid Kipper, was born at West Runton.

2 July 1788 Count Boruwlaski, the Polish dwarf who stood just 3ft 3in high, exhibited himself in Norwich.

3 July 1932 A Graf Zeppelin airship passed over Yarmouth and Norwich for the first time on her trip round Great Britain.

4 July 1825 Madame Tussaud's travelling exhibition of wax likenesses opened at the Assembly Rooms, Norwich.

5 July 1936 Sir Oswald Moseley addressed a Fascist meeting in Norwich Market Place.

6 July 1804 Mrs Bennett, the wife of an actor in the Norwich Company, gave birth to triplets.

7 July 1833 During a thunderstorm 'a fireball apparently about the size of a man's head' fell upon the thatched roof of the Black Tower on Butter Hills, Carrow, causing a fire that destroyed the astronomical observation equipment of a society of artisans.

8 July 1843 A whirlwind occurred at Blakeney carrying away several yards of flint wall and some smacks from the hatchings that it dumped on the marshes.

9 July 1940 The first air raid fatalities in Norwich took place during the Second World War.

10 July 1927 The first solo flight for the Norfolk and Norwich Aero Club was made on Mousehold by Mr W. Moore of Yarmouth.

11 July 1968 A severe storm swept over the county bringing down power lines, putting 1,100 telephones out of service and causing damage to the harbours at Brancaster, Overy Staithe and Wells.

12 July 1859 The new 'marine promenade' at Wells, built by the Earl of Leicester, was opened. The completed embankment measured 1 mile 132 yards long and stood 22ft 6in at its highest part.

13 July 1806 When two Yarmouth servant girls, wives of privates in the Shropshire Militia, were refused permission to return with them, the girls tied themselves together with ribbon, waded out to sea and drowned themselves.

14 July 1835 Handbills advertised a display of gymnastics by Mynheer Kousewinkler van Raachboomstadt 'The Dutch Hercules' on Chapel Field Gardens. Thousands turned up only to discover it was a hoax.

15 July 1863 The Maharajah Duleep Singh, the new owner of the Elveden Estate, arrived at Thetford to inspect his property.

16 July 1887 A new prison was built to replace the old Norwich Castle Prison (for Norfolk felons), and the Old Norwich City Gaol was opened on Knox Road, Norwich.

17 July 1923 Suckling House was presented to the city as a memorial to the late James Stuart by the Misses Colman.

18 July 1761 The first edition of the *Norfolk Chronicle* was published.

19 July 1951 The last execution was conducted in Norfolk. Dennis Moore and Alfred Reynolds went jointly to the gallows at HMP Norwich.

20 July 1879 An inundation of rain caused the Yare to overflow and thousands of acres of marsh flooded between Norwich and Yarmouth. Most of the county's hay crop was ruined by the wet weather.

21 July 1868 Chang the Chinese Giant was on display at the Old Corn Hall, Great Yarmouth. Advertised as the largest man in the world, it was claimed Chang stood nearly 9ft tall.

22 July 1948 Field Marshals Karl Gerd von Rundstedt and Erich von Manstein were released from captivity and left Diss for Germany.

23 July 1785 General Money made a balloon ascent from the Ranelagh Gardens, Norwich, but was blown out to sea and was fortunately rescued by the revenue cutter *Argus*.

24 July 1842 The death took place of John Sell Cotman, watercolourist and leading member of the Norwich School of Artists.

25 July 1995 Closed-circuit cameras observing the streets of Norwich were officially switched on for the first time.

26 July 1949 Queen drummer Roger Taylor was born at Dersingham.

27 July 1879 A deep crater of some 24 yards circumference appeared in a field near Attleborough. It was believed to have been caused by recent heavy rains.

28 July 1823 John Locke of Larling died aged 110. He left behind him a total of 130 children and grandchildren.

29 July 1844 The first appearance took place of the dwarf 'Tom Thumb' (Charles Stratton) at Norwich, where he appeared at the Theatre Royal courtesy of Mr P.T. Barnum the showman.

30 July 1900 Norwich Electric Tramways opened. 25,000 persons travelled on trams for the first time on this day.

31 July 1892 The unstable old tower of Hindolveston church collapsed carrying a large part of the nave with it.

AUGUST

1 August 1898 The most destructive fire to occur in Norwich burned down a number of business premises on Dove Street and the public library. By a curious coincidence on exactly the same day 104 years later Norwich Central Library also burned down.

2 August 1861 The celebrated tightrope walker Blondin made his first appearance at Norwich in a field on Newmarket Road where he walked a rope fixed about 60ft above the ground.

3 August 1932 The Floral Hall on Britannia Pier, Great Yarmouth, burned down.

4 August 1914 The outbreak of the First World War was announced across the county at 11.00 p.m.

5 August 1931 A severe thunderstorm took place over the county causing flooding, notably Bridge Street in Thetford where the water was recorded as being 18in deep at one point.

6 August 1857 Robert Bunn ran a mile against time on the Ipswich Road for a wager of £25. He accomplished the feat in 4 minutes and 30 seconds.

7 August 1862 Royal Assent was given for the formation of the Great Eastern Railway Company.

8 August 1931 A whirlwind at Mattishall and Mattishall Burgh occurred. Telegraph poles were broken, roofs stripped and a stack blown away.

9 August 1843 A severe storm raged over Norwich and Norfolk. The city flooded and extensive damage was inflicted upon glass by the accompanying hail and ice particles.

10 August 1835 Frances Billing and Catherine Frarey, 'The Burnham Poisoners', were executed in front of Norwich Castle. This would be the last public double execution and last execution of women in Norfolk.

11 August 1876 A great fire took place at Boulton & Paul's Ironworks in Norwich and about £10,000 of damage was caused.

12 August 1945 Nearly 200 children sent to Canada during the war returned to Norwich after five years away.

13 August 1815 A serious fire broke out near the church of St Lawrence, Norwich. Six houses were destroyed.

14 August 1802 News reached Norfolk of the first vessel to arrive at Brussels displaying the British flag; it was a pleasure yacht from Lynn and drew a large crowd of curious spectators.

15 August 1945 VJ Day celebrations took place across Norfolk for the end of the war in the Far East where many Norfolk men were serving or enduring captivity as prisoners of war in Japanese hands.

16 August 1936 Over 100 tons of cliffs fell at the eastern end of Sheringham.

17 August 1850 The death occurred of Hannah Sarah Hancock; born at St Helen's, Norwich, in 1781. She compiled a dictionary for children when she was just eight years old.

18 August 1909 PC Charles Alger of Great Yarmouth Borough Police was the first Norfolk police constable to be fatally shot in the line of duty.

19 August 1738 William Gotts, having been found guilty of horse theft at the Norfolk Assizes, was publicly hanged upon the Norwich Castle Hill gallows.

20 August 1698 A duel was fought on Cawston Heath between Sir Henry Hobart of Blickling Hall and Oliver le Neve of Great Witchingham. Hobart was mortally wounded and died later; Le Neve fled to Holland.

21 August 1821 Giovanni Battista Belzoni, the celebrated Venetian explorer and discoverer of Egyptian antiquities, stayed with Mr Jeremiah Ives at his residence on St Catherine's Hill, where several gentlemen of the city were invited to meet him.

22 August 1877 The foundation stone of the Hunstanton Convalescent Home was laid by the Countess of Leicester.

23 August 1768 Sir Astley Paston Cooper, eminent surgeon and anatomist, was born at Brooke Hall.

24 August 1549 Kett and his rebels were driven from the walls of the city by a military force led by John Dudley, Earl of Warwick.

25 August 1857 Norwich horse trainer William Feek jumped a high fence on Newmarket Road without touching it, his mount thus demonstrating a spring from point to point of 34ft.

26 August 1867 The last public execution at Norwich Castle took place. Hubbard Lingley had murdered his uncle Benjamin Black.

27 August 1912 Norwich and Norfolk suffered the worst deluge of rain on record with 7½in of rainfall over the previous 48 hours.

28 August 1643 The first day of the Siege of King's Lynn during the Civil War took place.

29 August 1959 Following amalgamation with the Suffolk Regiment, the regimental flag of the Royal Norfolk Regiment was lowered for the last time at Britannia Barracks, Norwich.

30 August 1847 The foundation stone was laid for the Lakenham viaduct.

31 August 1935 Norwich City FC's new football ground was opened on Carrow Road by Mr Russell Colman, Lord Lieutenant of Norfolk.

SEPTEMBER

1 September 1939 Evacuees from London began arriving in Norfolk.

2 September 1756 Fourteen French prisoners of war escaped from the Tolhouse Gaol at Great Yarmouth. Only four were recaptured.

3 September 1939 Thousands of Norfolk people clustered around their radios to hear the Prime Minister, Neville Chamberlain, declare the outbreak of the Second World War at 11.00 a.m.

4 September 1882 Frances Murphy, the founder of the Blue Ribbon temperance movement, inspired over 10,000 to sign the pledge during a three-week campaign in Norwich.

5 September 1936 The new Christian Spiritualist Church opened on Chapel Field North, Norwich.

6 September 1935 Norwich City Council erected the first Belisha Beacons in the city.

7 September 1931 The first cinema organ in Norwich was installed at the Haymarket Picture House.

8 September 1910 The City of Norwich School, Eaton, was opened by the Revd Hon. Edward Lyttelton, Headmaster of Eton.

9 September 1888 The majority of the Orchard Street Saw Mills, Norwich, were destroyed by fire.

10 September 1874 The Thorpe Railway Disaster took place. Two trains collided head-on at Thorpe St Andrew. Both drivers and firemen were killed, as were seventeen passengers with four later dying from their injuries.

11 September 1843 The Earl of Leicester laid the foundation stone of the new quay at Wells.

12 September 1876 A case of fireworks in the bar exploded aboard the *Alexandra* steamer chartered for a works outing from Pockthorpe Brewery. The cabin filled with fumes and four deaths resulted.

13 September 1920 Mrs J.E. Stuart took her seat as the first woman JP for Norwich.

14 September 1856 A white stork was shot in the plantation of Mr R.H. Saye at North Pickenham.

15 September 1819 A prizefight was held between Barlee the Berg Apton Groom and Belasco on Tasburgh Common and was attended by 8–10,000 men and women. Forty-one rounds were fought, and Belasco was the eventual victor.

16 September 1843 A platform was erected atop Norwich Cathedral spire by a team of sappers to support a temporary observatory for the purposes of the Ordnance Survey.

17 September 1852 Mr S. Chamber RN made a balloon ascent from the Vauxhall Gardens, Yarmouth, and descended on Mautby marshes.

18 September 1852 John Thurston, labourer, died at Saham Toney in his 105th year.

19 September 1876 A roller-skating rink built for £9,000 was opened at St Giles Street with an outer rink abutting Bethel Street, Norwich.

20 September 1720 A mob rioted in Pockthorpe, Norwich, 'under the pretence of destroying calicoes'. It was dispersed by the local artillery company.

21 September 2005 The Chapelfield shopping complex opened.

22 September 1900 The body of a woman was found strangled with a bootlace on the South Beach at Great Yarmouth. Her husband, Herbert Bennett, was found guilty and executed at HMP Norwich in 1901.

23 September 1939 Cricket commentator Henry 'Blowers' Blofeld was born at Hoveton Home Farm.

24 September 1882 Charles John Palmer FSA, best known for his *Perlustration of Great Yarmouth* and thrice mayor of the borough, died at Great Yarmouth.

25 September 1851 A severe gale occurred off the Norfolk coast and caused much damage to shipping at Great Yarmouth.

26 September 1856 Unprecedented amounts of herring were caught off Yarmouth. Over the previous three weeks boats, reached the daily average of 100 lasts or 1,320,000 fish.

27 September 1766 A dreadful riot in Norwich took place on account of the great scarcity and price of provisions, especially corn.

28 September 1799 The 'Grand Old' Duke of York's army landed at Yarmouth upon its return from an unsuccessful campaign in Holland. They consisted of Guards and twenty-four other regiments amounting to some 25,000 infantry and cavalry troops.

29 September 1758 Nelson was born at Burnham Thorpe Rectory.

30 September 1851 The opening of Norwich waterworks was publicly celebrated.

OCTOBER

1 October 1998 An international pipeline connecting Bacton to Zeebrugge for the transport of gas was opened.

2 October 1766 Loyal citizens of Norwich restored calm to the city by opposing rioters protesting about the scarcity and expense of grain.

3 October 1944 A V2 rocket fell on Hellesdon golf course.

4 October 1956 The first broadcasts took place from the new BBC Broadcasting House on All Saint's Green, Norwich.

5 October 1510 John Caius born at Norwich. He went on to become President of the College of Physicians nine times and physician to Edward VI, Queen Mary and Queen Elizabeth.

6 October 1799 French prisoner of war escapee Lieutenant Jean de Narde was shot out of a tree at East Dereham.

7 October 1852 The Priory Schools were opened at Great Yarmouth by the Bishop of Norwich.

8 October 1927 Norwich War Memorial was unveiled by Bertie Withers, a private who had been severely wounded while serving with 4th Battalion, the Norfolk Regiment.

9 October 1875 The foundation stone of Yarmouth Aquarium was laid by Lord Suffield.

10 October 1970 Sir Matthew Pinsent, winner of ten world championship gold medals and four consecutive Olympic gold medals during his rowing career, was born at Holt.

11 October 1859 Dickens gave readings at St Andrew's Hall, Norwich.

12 October 1915 Norfolk's greatest heroine, Nurse Edith Cavell, daughter of the Rector of Swardeston, was executed at the Tir Nationale, Belgium, by a German firing squad.

13 October 1861 The death occurred of Sir William Cubitt, Dilham-born master engineer and inventor of the prison treadwheel.

14 October 1867 An elephant from Edmond's Menagerie fell over in Denmark Street, Diss, and despite the best efforts of all concerned, she died the following day.

15 October 1843 The death occurred of the famous Great Yarmouth Tolhouse prison visitor Sarah Martin.

16 October 1864 The 3,200-ton screw steamer *Ontario* was stranded on Happisburgh Sands on her maiden voyage from Shields to Alexandria.

17 October 1859 Attleborough was lit by gas for the first time. This event was celebrated by a public dinner at the New Inn.

18 October 1832 It was reported that of the 320 cases of cholera declared in Norfolk since 5 April, 128 had resulted in death.

19 October 1971 World Heavyweight boxing champion Muhammad Ali visited Norwich to open a supermarket on St Stephen's Street as part of a promotional tour for Ovaltine.

20 October 1874 The East Norfolk Railway from Norwich to North Walsham opened for traffic.

21 October 1930 A new bridge over Yarmouth Haven was opened by Edward, Prince of Wales.

22 October 1867 An immense eel was taken from the River Ouse, near Denver Sluice, measuring 5ft 8in in length and weighing 36lb.

23 October 1940 Fire broke out in the early hours of the morning at the Back of the Inns in Norwich. Hotel buildings and shops were destroyed in the Royal Arcade and White Lion Street.

24 October 1415 Norfolk man, Sir Thomas Erpingham led the English archers to victory at the Battle of Agincourt.

25 October 1909 King Edward VII paid what was to be his last official visit to Norwich.

26 October 1882 A seventeen-year-old girl sleepwalked from the home of her employer at Felthorpe to Cawston, a distance of 5 miles. When revived she had no recollection of having left her bed.

27 October 1947 Henry Blogg GC retired after 38 years as coxswain of the Cromer lifeboat. He had served a total of 53 years as crewman and coxswain.

28 October 1838 The first meeting of the Chartist movement to take place in Norfolk was held on this day in Norwich Market Place.

29 October 1938 The new Norwich City Hall was opened by King George VI and Queen Elizabeth.

30 October 1910 General Baden Powell inspected Boy Scouts at the Drill Hall, Norwich.

31 October 1823 A violent storm occurred over the county, resulting in a coastline strewn with wrecks and many lives lost.

NOVEMBER

1 November 1929 The R101 airship passed over Norwich on her trial flight.

2 November 1801 The Prince of Orange landed at Great Yarmouth and stayed until the 6th when he sailed aboard the packet *Diana* for Cuxhaven.

3 November 1579 John Stubbs, Buxton-born puritan and zealot, had his right hand cut off in Westminster Market Place for publishing a pamphlet criticising the proposed marriage of Elizabeth I and the Duke of Anjou.

4 November 1931 The bells of St Giles' Church, Norwich, were taken down due to the ravages of death watch beetles.

5 November 1866 Little Walsingham church organ was blown to pieces by a gunpowder charge.

6 November 1852 Rear Admiral Black, one of the oldest officers in the Royal Navy, died at Ormesby in his eighty-second year.

7 November 1845 Trowse Swing Bridge swung over the river for the first time. After passing government inspection the first train passed over the bridge on 15 December 1845.

8 November 1934 The Lord Mayor of Norwich opened a new fire station on Bethel Street.

9 November 1923 Miss Ethel Colman was appointed first Lady Lord Mayor of Norwich.

10 November 1888 Gorleston lifeboat, *The Refuge*, capsized while on salvage service; four of her crew drowned.

11 November 1918 Armistice Day, the end of the First World War, took place.

12 November 1949 A big fire at Great Yarmouth destroyed the North Quay warehouses of Norton Bros.

13 November 1801 Sergeant Peter Donohue of 30th Foot was the last man to be hanged at King's Lynn. He was hanged for uttering counterfeit Bank of England notes.

14 November 1993 A 100-ton Tayjack 1 rig broke from its moorings in a severe storm and smashed through Cromer pier.

15 November 1828 A hamper being carried by Marsh & Swan's London van from King's Lynn was found to contain the body of a young woman thought to have been removed from a grave in the town by bodysnatchers.

16 November 1846 The first recorded canary show was held at Norwich at the Greyhound Inn, Ber Street, when 300 specimens belonging to the canary club were exhibited.

17 November 1888 There was panic in Yarmouth after a letter was received by Great Yarmouth police purporting to come from Jack the Ripper threatening to 'rip up two Norwich women'.

18 November 1936 A gale caused wrecks around the Norfolk coast; Gorleston lifeboat was damaged.

19 November 1929 The first automatic telephone exchange in Norwich District was opened at Fundenhall.

20 November 1881 Hannah Brett was murdered at Saham Toney by recently released convict Henry Stebbings.

21 November 1875 A Scottish fisherman named Watson successfully climbed the figure of Britannia atop the Nelson column at Great Yarmouth. He then descended via the lightning conductor on the outside and achieved this all while under the influence of drink!

22 November 1863 Robert Hales, the celebrated Norfolk Giant, died on this day aged forty-three. In his prime he stood 7ft 6in tall, measured 64in around the waist and weighed 33 stone.

23 November 1950 The Assembly House, Norwich, was restored and given to the city by Mr H.J. Sexton and opened as an arts centre.

24 November 1864 The 530-ton screw steamer *William Hutt* was lost in a severe gale off Yarmouth with the loss of sixteen hands.

25 November 1998 The new Norwich Crown Court was opened.

26 November 1838 North Walsham was lit by gas for the very first time. A band played around the town and a dinner was held at the King's Arms Hotel to celebrate.

27 November 1947 Salt tide reached Hoveton and resulted in masses of dead fish in the Thurne and Bure.

28 November 1848 The infamous 'Stanfield Hall Murders' of the Recorder of Norwich and his son were committed by James Blomfield Rush.

29 November 1830 A mob destroyed the sawmill at Catton and looms at Willett's Factory in St Martin's, Norwich. 200 Chelsea Pensioners were called out in the city to help preserve the peace.

30 November 1888 Walsoken murderer Robert Goodale's head was torn off during his execution by hanging at Norwich Castle. Executioner James Berry was officiating and was acquitted of any fault.

DECEMBER

1 December 1980 The opening night of the Norwich Puppet theatre took place with a performance of *Humbug, Humbug,* an interpretation of Dickens' *A Christmas Carol.*

2 December 1853 Noted author and socialite-turned-Quaker Amelia Opie died at her residence on Castle Meadow, Norwich.

3 December 1923 The new Regent Theatre was formally opened on Prince of Wales Road, Norwich.

4 December 1314 Black Death hit Norwich and hundreds died.

5 December 1896 Apprentice Albert Delves was killed when his clothes became entangled and he was drawn into a machine at St Mary's Silk Mills, Norwich.

6 December 1927 The Electricity Committee inaugurated a service to North Walsham.

7 December 1549 Robert Kett, the leader of the Norfolk Rebellion, was executed and gibbeted upon the walls of Norwich Castle.

8 December 1910 The Roman Catholic Church of St John the Baptist on Earlham Road, Norwich, was opened.

9 December 1808 Mary Hudson made good her escape from Norwich City Gaol carrying her six-month-old baby with her. There is no record of her recapture.

10 December 1935 The last tram service was run in Norwich.

11 December 1851 A horde of 4,000 Roman coins in an urn were ploughed up at Easton.

12 December 1899 A new organ was erected in Norwich Cathedral at a cost of £6,000.

13 December 1933 The valiant rescue of the crew of the barge *Sepoy* was carried out by the Cromer lifeboat under Coxswain Henry Blogg. This dramatic service was visible off Cromer and large crowds gathered on the cliffs to watch it.

14 December 1970 Beth Orton, singer-songwriter, was born at East Dereham.

15 December 1880 A new warehouse at Lynn Docks was destroyed by fire. The damage was estimated at £15,000.

16 December 1801 Stratton Strawless old hall was destroyed by fire.

17 December 1994 3,000 people marched down Chapelfield in Norwich to protest over the closure of the Nestlé chocolate factory.

18 December 1882 A large portion of Gunton Hall, the seat of Lord Suffield, was destroyed by fire.

19 December 1897 Typhoid fever at King's Lynn was caused by impurity in the water supply. Breaking out in October, by this period there had been 440 cases and 43 deaths.

20 December 1921 Stranger's Hall and its contents were presented to the city by Mr L.G. Bolingbroke.

21 December 1862 Sea broke over the sandhills at Wells flooding 700 acres of the west marshes.

22 December 1809 Sir George Edward Paget, physician and a Regius professor of physics at Cambridge, was born at Great Yarmouth.

23 December 1876 William Cooke Stafford, one of the oldest journalists in the country, died at Norwich aged eighty-three.

24 December 1818 A tradesman at Beeston-next-Mileham made a wager he would carry 12 stone of flour a distance of 10 miles in six hours; a task that he achieved in 5¼ hours.

25 December 1836 Christmas Day was ushered in with severe snow and hail storms. All traffic was stopped. The Ipswich Mail coach that should have arrived on this day did not reach Norwich until 29 December.

26 December 1856 Boxing Day was observed in Norwich as a general holiday for the first time.

27 December 1855 Mr W. Shalders, inventor of the fountain pump, died at Norwich in his eightieth year.

28 December 1886 Considerable damage was caused to telephone lines in Norwich by a fall of heavy stone.

29 December 1914 A fierce gale caused much damage across the city and county.

30 December 1823 The extensive chalk workings discovered some 35ft beneath the surface, near St Giles' Gates, were illuminated by coloured lamps and opened for public inspection.

31 December 1808 Boxing legends John Gulley, Tom Cribb and Tom Belcher gave a boxing exhibition at Norwich before an audience of 800.

SELECT BIBLIOGRAPHY

It really would be a very unwieldy bibliography to list every book I have consulted for a fascinating fact or snippet for this volume, but I feel some books I have found useful or those that would be helpful to readers should, in the spirit of this publication, be listed:

Brookes, Pamela, *Norfolk Miscellany* (Derby, 2009)
Browne, Philip, *The History of Norwich* (Norwich, 1814)
Daynes, J., *The History of Norwich* (Norwich, 1848)
Dew, Walton N., *A Dyshe of Norfolke Dumplings* (London, 1898)
Forby, Robert, *The Vocabulary of East Anglia* (London, 1830)
Glyde, John, *The Norfolk Garland* (London, 1872)
Hudson, the Revd William and Tingey, John Cottingham, *The Records of the City of Norwich* (Norwich, 1906)
Mackie, Charles, *Norfolk Annals*, 2 vols (Norwich, 1901)
Mardle, Jonathan (foreword by), *Broad Norfolk* (Norwich, 1949)
Matchett, J. (ed.), *The Norfolk and Norwich Remembrancer and Vade-Mecum* (Norwich, 1822)
Ogley, Bob, Davisdon, Mark and Currie, Ian, *The Norfolk and Suffolk Weather Book* (Westerham, 1993)
Palmer, Frederick Danby, *Yarmouth Notes* (Yarmouth, 1889)
Rawcliffe, Carole and Wilson, Richard (eds), *Medieval Norwich* (London, 2004)
——, *Norwich Since 1550* (London, 2004)
Rye, Walter, *Tourist's Guide to Norfolk* (London, 1892)
Skipper, Keith, *Hidden Norfolk* (Newbury, 1998)
——, *How to Survive in Norfolk* (Halsgrove, 2007)
Storey, Neil R., *A Grim Almanac of Norfolk* (Stroud, 2003)
——, *Hanged at Norwich* (Stroud, 2011)

Kelly's Directory of Norfolk
Norfolk Fair
Eastern Daily Press
Norfolk Fair
The Times
Observer

White's Directory of Norfolk
East Anglian Magazine
Norfolk Chronicle
Norwich Mercury
Daily Express
Yarmouth Mercury